Budgeting, pricing and Cost Controls
Charles Woelfel

———————
—————————

To Colette

—————————
———————

Preface

Budgeting, Pricing & Cost Controls: A Desktop Encyclopedia is a significant sourcebook and reference for managers, executives, accountants, consultants, academicians, and graduate students. Concepts related to management, production, finance, economics, and accounting are discussed in detail and cross-referenced to provide the reader with easy access to related topics. This one-volume, state-of-the-art encyclopedia is a comprehensive, accurate, and convenient source of management information that is available at one's fingertips. It provides an update on contemporary trends in managing, planning, controlling, budgeting, and pricing. It offers a current analysis of basic management functions including:

Managing	Decision making
Setting goals and objectives	Budgeting
Planning	Forecasting
Controlling	Pricing
Organizing	Negotiating
Directing	Delegating
Motivating	Understanding organi-
Evaluating	zational behavior
Communicating	Maintaining quality control
Leading	

The encyclopedia focuses on basic objectives:

1. It establishes a balance between management theory and management objectives.
2. It effectively relates management theory to management practice.
3. It offers a contemporary view of how a business can be organized and managed.
4. It deals constructively with many of the problems managers and other decision makers must solve.
5. It serves as a practical guide to applying modern management theory to solving everyday problems.
6. It emphasizes the importance of establishing goals and objectives as the basis of the planning, controlling, and evaluating processes.

Difficult, complex, and significant management topics are presented clearly, understandably, and authoritatively. This encyclopedia is conveniently alphabetized and indexed for easy reference. Each of the entries is cross-referenced to provide easy access to related concepts. Most of the entries contain bibliographies which lead to primary and secondary sources. Numerous exhibits are used throughout the book to clarify important concepts.

Many major analytical procedures associated with financial planning, controlling, and decision making are included in the encyclopedia. The analytical procedures are carefully described and illustrated with meaningful examples. These procedures include:

Return-on-investment analysis
Break-even analysis
Contribution margin analysis
Opportunity cost analysis
Incremental cost analysis
Financial statement analysis
Benefit-cost analysis
Distribution (marketing) cost analysis
Variance analysis
Game theory
Linear programming
Learning curves

This book is designed and written for a selective audience who must have immediate access to authoritative management information on a day-to-day basis:

Managers and executives
> Top management
> Middle-level management
> Operating management

Managers of small, medium size, and large businesses and not-for-profit organizations

CEOs

Corporate officers and directors

Sole proprietors

Controllers

Financial planners

Financial managers

Accountants

Business educators

Behavioral scientists

Operations researchers

Forecasters

Statisticians

Industrial engineers

The author wishes to express his appreciation for the assistance and encouragement provided by Probus Publishing Company throughout this project.

Contents

Contents

Contents

ACCOUNTING

Accounting is an information system which accumulates, processes, and communicates information, primarily financial in nature, about a specific economic entity.

The American Accounting Association defined accounting in a Statement of Basic Theory, 1966, as follows:

"Accounting is the process of identifying, measuring and communicating economic information to permit informed judgments and decisions by users of the information.... The objectives of accounting are to provide for the following purposes:

1. Making decisions concerning the use of limited resources, including crucial decision areas, and determination of goals and objectives.

2. Effectively directing and controlling an organization's human and material resources.

3. Maintaining and reporting on the custodianship of resources.

4. Facilitating social functions and controls."

This definition identifies the major role of accounting as providing information for those who use the information. The definition specifies three major functions of accounting: identifying, measuring, and communicating economic information.

In 1970 the Accounting Principles Board of the American Institute of Certified Public Accountants developed the following definition of accounting:

> "Accounting is a service activity. Its function is to provide quantitative information, primarily financial in nature, about economic activities that is intended to be useful in making economic decisions—in making reasoned choices among alternative courses of action."

The definition of accounting is goal-oriented rather than process-oriented or function-oriented. It emphasizes economic decision-making activities rather than the functions of accounting as the major objectives of accounting.

In a popular sense, accounting has been referred to as *the language of business*, since it is the basic tool for recording and reporting economic events and transactions that affect business enterprises. Other concepts view accounting as a historical record, a mirror of current economic reality, a subset of a total business information system, or as a commodity that is the product of economic activity.

Accounting equation. The accounting equation expresses the relationship that exists between assets, liabilities, and owners' equity. In its simplest form, the accounting equation can be represented as follows:

ASSETS − LIABILITIES = OWNERS' EQUITY

The accounting equation in terms of net assets is

ASSETS − LIABILITIES = NET ASSETS

The accounting equation states an equality and establishes a relationship among the three major accounting elements. Owners' equity is shown as the residual of assets over liabilities, which also equals "net assets." The accounting equation can be restated in this form:

ASSETS = LIABILITIES + OWNERS' EQUITY

When the accounting equation is expressed in this format, owners and creditors are shown as having claims against the assets of the enterprise. The accounting equation can also be expressed in a format that combines liabilities and owners' equity into a single concept referred to as *equities*:

ASSETS = EQUITIES

Accounting functions. Accounting deals with numbers and measurable quantities. The accounting system accumulates, measures, and communicates numbers and measurable quantities of economic information about an enterprise. These three functions can be represented as a flow of information from source to destination as follows:

| ACCUMULATION | --→ | MEASUREMENT | --→ | COMMUNICATION |

Accumulation refers primarily to recording and classifying data in journals and ledgers. The accounting system accumulates data relating primarily to completed transactions and events. Measurement refers to the quantification of business transactions or other economic events that have occurred or that may occur. Measurement determines how to select the best amounts to recognize in the financial statements. The accounting system communicates relevant and reliable information to investors, creditors, managers, and others for internal and external decision making.

Accounting period. Custom as well as income tax and other legal considerations has focused on annual reporting periods and an annual accounting cycle. A reporting period that begins on January 1 and ends on December 31 is referred to as a *calendar – year* accounting period. Any other beginning and ending period of one year is called a *fiscal – year*. The accounting period should be clearly identified on the financial statements.

In selecting an annual reporting period, some entities adopt a period that ends when operations are at a low point in order to simplify year-end accounting procedures and permit more rapid preparation of financial statements. At such a date, inventories and accounts receivable will normally be at their lowest point. Such an accounting period is referred to as *natural business year* since it conforms to the natural annual cycle of the entity.

Financial reports for periods shorter than one year, such as quarterly reports, are referred to as *interim reports* or *interim statements*.

For income tax purposes, the accounting period is usually a year. Unless a fiscal year is chosen, taxpayers must determine their tax liability by using the calendar year as the period of measurement. A change in accounting period requires the approval of the Internal Revenue Service.

See also Objectives of financial reporting; Elements of financial statements; Qualitative characteristics of accounting information; Accounting principles; Financial statements; Accounting basis; Accounting controls; Accounting policies and procedures; Measurement.

REFERENCES
Carey, John L., *Getting Acquainted with Accounting* (Houghton Mifflin, Boston, 1973).
Seidler, Lee, and Carmichael, D. R., eds., *Accountants' Handbook* (John Wiley & Sons, New York, 1981).
Nicherson, Clarence B., *Accounting Handbook for Nonaccountants* (Van Nostrand Reinhold, New York, 1985).

ACCOUNTING ASSUMPTIONS

Accounting assumptions are those broad concepts that underlie generally accepted accounting principles and serve as a foundation for these principles. Accounting assumptions are statements accepted without proof that also serve as the basis for accounting activities. The major accounting assumptions include the following: the business entity assumption, the continuity assumption, the periodic and timely reporting assumption, and the monetary unit assumption.

A basic assumption in accounting is that economic activity can be identified with a particular unit or entity of accountability. This unit or entity is the one to be accounted for. The business entity assumption determines the nature and scope of the reporting that is required for the unit or entity. The entity for accounting purposes is identified as the economic unit that controls resources, incurs obligations, and otherwise is involved in directing economic activities which relate to a specific accountability unit. Accounting units or entities include corporations, partnerships, proprietorships, not-for-profit entities, trusts, and others.

Accounting is based on the assumption that the accounting unit or entity is engaged in continuous and ongoing activities. The accounting unit or entity is assumed to remain in operation into the foreseeable future to achieve its goals and objectives. This assumption is referred to as the continuity or going-concern assumption.

The continuous operations of a business or other economic unit or entity over an extended period of time can be meaningfully segmented into equal time periods, such as a year, quarter, or month. The periodic and timely reporting assumptions require that accounting reporting should be done periodically and on a timely basis so that it is relevant and reliable.

The monetary unit assumption requires that financial information be measured and accounted for in the basic monetary unit of the country in which the enterprise is located (dollars for U.S. firms). The monetary value of an economic event or transaction, determined at the time it is recorded, is not adjusted for subsequent changes in the purchasing power of the monetary unit (as occurs in periods of inflation or deflation).

See also Accounting; Accounting principles; Accounting policies and procedures; Financial statements.

REFERENCE
Smith, Jay M., and Skousen, K. Fred, *Intermediate Accounting* (South-Western, Cincinnati, OH, 1984).

ACCOUNTING BASIS

Major bases of accounting include the accrual, cash, and modified cash bases. In accrual accounting, revenue and gains are recognized in the period they are earned. Expenses and losses are recognized in the period they are incurred. Accrual accounting is concerned with the economic consequences of events and transactions instead of merely with cash receipts and cash payments. Under accrual accounting, net income does not necessarily reflect cash receipts and cash payments for a time period. Accrual accounting generally provides the best measure of earnings, earning power, managerial performance, and stewardship.

Cash-basis accounting recognizes only transactions involving actual cash receipts and disbursements occurring in a given period. Cash-basis accounting recognizes revenues and gains when cash is received and expenses and losses when cash is paid. No attempt is made to record unpaid bills or amounts owed to or by the entity. Cash-basis accounting is generally deficient as an accounting model that attempts to produce a statement of financial position and an income statement. However, cash-basis accounting is widely used for income tax purposes.

Under a modified cash basis of accounting, certain expenditures would be capitalized and amortized in the future. For example, under cash-basis accounting, the purchase of equipment for cash is expensed immediately; under a modified cash basis, the purchase is recorded as an asset. A portion of the acquisition cost is later recognized as an expense when the services of the asset are consumed.

To illustrate the difference between the accrual basis and the cash basis of accounting, assume the following data. A company is engaged in a service business. During 1990 the company billed its customers for $100,000 for services performed during 1990. These billings resulted in cash payments to the company of $80,000 in 1990 and $20,000 in 1991. The company incurred expenses of $70,000 while carrying out these services during 1990. The company paid out $40,000 in cash on these expenses during 1990 and $30,000 in 1991. No other revenue or expense transactions occurred during 1990 or 1991.

| | Accrual Basis | | Cash Basis | |
	1990	1991	1990	1991
Revenue	$100,000	—	$80,000	$20,000
Expenses	70,000	—	40,000	30,000
Net income (loss)	$ 30,000	—	40,000	$(10,000)

Note that although the combined net income (loss) for the two years is the same, the amounts in the separate years differ. Accrual-basis accounting typically provides a better measure of net income than does cash-basis accounting.

To convert accrual-basis income to cash-basis income, certain adjustments must be made for all noncash charges and credits contained in accrual-basis net income. Cash from operations can be conceptualized as follows:

Cash from operations = Cash collected from customers − Cash paid for inventory purchases − Cash paid for expenses

or

Cash from operations = Net income on accrual basis + Accounting charges not requiring cash outlays − Accounting credits not providing cash

A

Net income from operations computed according to generally accepted accounting principles can be converted to cash flow from operations according to the following general procedures:

Net income from operations
Plus: Items reducing income but not using cash, such as depreciation, depletion, and amortization expenses
        Decreases in current assets other than cash
        Increases in current liabilities
Less: Increases in current assets other than cash
        Decreases in current liabilities
Equals: Cash flow from operations

See Exhibit A-1 for an illustration of how accrual-basis accounting statements can be adjusted to cash-basis statements.

Exhibit A–1
Converting Net Income from Operations to Cash Flow from Operations

Net income from operations		$20,000
Add:		
Items reducing income but not using cash:		
Depreciation, building and equipment	$20,000	
Amortization, patent	10,000	30,000
Decreases in current assets other than cash:		
Accounts receivable	$15,000	
Prepaid expenses	5,000	20,000
Increases in current liabilities:		
Accounts payable	$10,000	
Accrued liabilities	5,000	15,000
Subtotal		85,000
Deduct:		
Increases in current assets other than cash:		
Inventories	$15,000	
Decreases in current liabilities:		
Wages payable	5,000	20,000
Cash flow from operations		$65,000

See also Accounting.

REFERENCE
Smith, Jay M., and Skousen, K. Fred, *Intermediate Accounting* (South-Western, Cincinnati, OH, 1984).

ACCOUNTING CONTROLS
Accounting controls include the plan of organization and the procedures and records dealing with the broad objectives of safeguarding assets and improving the reliability of financial records required for the preparation of financial statements. Accounting controls are concerned primarily with systems of authorization and approval, controls over assets, internal auditing procedures, and other financial matters. It is management's responsibility to establish and maintain an appropriate system of internal accounting control.

According to Statements on Auditing Standards Nos. 1 and 30, the operative objectives of accounting controls are designed to provide reasonable assurance that:

1. Transactions are executed in accordance with management's general or specific authorization.

2. Transactions are recorded as necessary (1) to permit preparation of financial statements in conformity with generally accepted accounting principles or any other criteria applicable to such statements and (2) to maintain accountability for assets.

3. Access to assets is permitted only in accordance with management's authorization.

4. The recorded accountability for assets is compared with the existing assets at reasonable intervals and appropriate action is taken with respect to any differences.

A

Accounting control systems provide reasonable, not absolute, assurance that the accounting control objectives are met. The concept of reasonable assurance recognizes that accounting control systems are subject to cost-benefit constraints.

See also Administrative controls; Internal control; Control function; Fraud.

REFERENCES
Statement on Auditing Standard No. 1, "Codification of Auditing Standards and Procedures" (Commerce Clearing House, Chicago, Il, 1980).
Statement on Auditing Standard No. 30, "Reporting on Internal Accounting Control" (American Institute of Certified Public Accountants, New York).

ACCOUNTING POLICIES AND PROCEDURES

The accounting policies of a reporting entity are the specific accounting principles and the methods of applying those principles that are judged by the management of the enterprise to be the most appropriate in the circumstances to present fairly financial position, changes in financial position, and results of operations in accordance with generally accepted accounting principles and that have been adopted for preparing the financial statements. Information about the accounting policies adopted by a reporting enterprise is essential for financial statement users and should be disclosed. Accounting principles and their methods of application in the following areas are considered particularly important:

1. A selection from existing alternatives.

2. Areas that are peculiar to a particular industry in which the company operates.

3. Unusual and innovative applications of generally accepted accounting principles.

Examples of disclosures commonly required by a business enterprise include those relating to depreciation methods, inventory pricing, basis of consolidations, and recognition of profit on long-term, construction-type contracts.

The preferable place to disclose accounting policies is under the caption Summary of Significant Accounting Policies or as the initial note to the financial statements.

Accounting procedures are those rules and practices associated with the operations of an accounting system that lead to the development of financial statements. Accounting procedures include the methods, practices, and techniques used to carry out accounting objectives and to implement accounting principles. For example, LIFO, FIFO, and other inventory methods are accounting procedures as are various depreciation methods such as straight-line depreciation and accelerated depreciation. An accounting convention is an accounting procedure which does not have official approval by an authoritative body such as the Financial Accounting Standards Board.

Accounting procedures can vary from company to company and from industry to industry. An accounting procedure should be selected in a given circumstance if its use reflects generally accepted accounting principles and if it is appropriate to record, process, and report the event or transaction.

See also Accounting; Accounting principles.

REFERENCES
Kelly-Newton, Lauren, *Accounting Policy Formulation* (Addison-Wesley, Reading, MA, 1980).
APB No. 22, *Disclosure of Accounting Policies* (APB, 1972).

ACCOUNTING PRINCIPLES
Accounting principles are the guidelines, laws, or rules which are adopted by the accounting profession and which serves as guides to accounting practice. Accounting principles include the accounting and reporting assumptions, standards, and

practices that a company must use in preparing external financial statements. An objective of generally accepted accounting principles (GAAP) is to reduce the differences and inconsistencies in accounting practice, thereby improving the comparability and credibility of financial reports.

The phrase "generally accepted accounting principles," or GAAP, is a technical term that identifies the conventions, rules, and procedures that represent accepted accounting practice at a particular period of time. GAAP reflect a consensus of what professionals consider good accounting practices and procedures. GAAP are prescribed by authoritative bodies, such as the Financial Accounting Standards Board. The term "principle" does not imply a rule or law from which there can be no deviation or exception. The application of generally accepted accounting principles typically requires the professional judgment of the accountant. Accounting principles are understood to have application primarily to material and significant items. Items with little or no consequence can usually be dealt with on a basis of expediency or practicality. The Accounting Principles Board stated that:

> "Generally accepted accounting principles incorporate the consensus at a particular time as to which economic resources and obligations should be recorded as assets and liabilities. . . which changes in assets and liabilities should be recorded, when these changes should be recorded, how the recorded assets and liabilities and changes in them should be measured, what information should be disclosed, and which financial statements should be prepared."

Sources of generally accepted accounting principles include the following:

1. Pronouncements of the Financial Accounting Standards Board (FASB) and its predecessors, the Accounting Principles Board (APB) and the Committee on Accounting

Procedures (CAP). These pronouncements include FASB statements of Standards and Interpretations, APB Opinions, and American Institute of Certified Public Accountants (AICPA) Accounting Research Bulletins (ARB).

2. FASB Technical Bulletins and AICPA's Interpretations, Audit Guides, Accounting Guides, and Statements of Position.

3. General accounting practice.

4. Securities and Exchange Commission regulations.

5. Internal Revenue Service regulations.

6. Accounting literature.

Levels of authority of sources of accounting principles are determined according to the following hierarchy:

1. Pronouncements of authoritative bodies specified by Rule 203 of the AICPA Code of Professional Ethics. These include FASB Standards and Interpretations, APB Opinions, and CAP Accounting Research Bulletins. Deviations from these principles require an auditor to either qualify the opinion or explain the reasons and effects of the departures in the body of the audit report.

2. Pronouncements of bodies composed of expert accountants that follow a due process procedure. These include AICPA Industry Audit Guides and Accounting Guides and Statements of Position.

3. Pronouncements, or practices, that represent prevalent practice or application to specific circumstances of generally accepted pronouncements. These include FASB Technical Bulletins, AICPA Interpretations, and industry practices.

4. Other accounting literature. These include APB Statements, AICPA Issues Papers, FASB Concept Statements,
pronouncements of other professional associations or
regulatory agencies, and textbooks and journal articles.

When applying the scheme, work down from the top of the
classification described in the preceding paragraph until an
answer is found. Where an inconsistency between categories
exists, it is recommended that the rule suggested by the higher
level of authoritative literature shall prevail. In cases of a conflict between sources within a category, attempt to establish
which treatment better presents the substance of the transaction
given the specific circumstances.

Accounting principles are classifed as (1) measurement
principles and (2) disclosure principles. Measurement principles deal with quantifying accounting events, transactions,
and circumstance and determining the timing and basis of
items which impact the financial statements. Disclosure principles deal with matters which must be disclosed in the financial statements in order for the statements to be not misleading.

For recognition in financial statements, an item must
comply with the following criteria, subject to contraints of
materiality (the item must make a difference to a decision
maker) and benefit-cost (benefits must exceed costs):

1. Definition: the item must meet the definition of an
element in financial statements (elements include assets,
liabilities, revenue, gain, expense, loss, and others).

2. Measurability: the element must have an attribute
(historical cost, replacement cost, market value, present value, and net realizable value).

3. Relevance.

4. Reliability.

See also Accounting; Accounting assumptions; Accounting basis; Accounting policies and procedures; Financial statements.

REFERENCES
Committee to Prepare a Statement of Basic Accounting Theory, *A Statement of Basic Accounting Theory* (AAA, Evanston, IL, 1966).
Grady, Paul, *Inventory of Generally Accepted Accounting Principles for Business Enterprises* (American Institute of Certified Public Accountants, New York, 1965).
Meddaugh, E. James, *Guide to Professional Accounting Standards* (Prentice-Hall, Englewood Cliffs, NJ, 1983).

ADMINISTRATIVE CONTROLS

Administrative controls include the plan of organization and the procedures and records associated with the decision processes involved in management's authorization of transactions. Administrative controls are designed to facilitate management's responsibility for achieving the objectives of the organization and to improve operational efficiency and compliance with management's policies. Administrative controls are the basis for establishing the accounting control over transactions. Administrative controls can be contrasted with accounting controls (see Accounting controls). Examples contrasting administrative and accounting controls are illustrated here:

Accounting Controls	Administrative Controls
Cash	
Cash receipts are to be deposited daily; all cash disbursements are to be made by check.	Use cash forecasts to determine short-term borrowing requirements.
Inventory	
The perpetual inventory method is to be used to account for inventory.	Inventory modeling techniques are to be used to determine the quantity of inventory to order and the timing of orders.

See also Accounting controls; Internal control; Fraud.

REFERENCE
Statement on Auditing Standard No. 30, "Reporting on Internal Accounting Control"(American Institute of Certified Public Accountants, New York.)

ALLOCATION
Allocation is generally considered to be the accounting process of assigning or distributing an amount according to a plan or a formula. Allocation problems arise in many situations which involve accounting, including the following:

1. reducing an amount by periodic payments or write-downs:

    a. reducing a liability which arose as a result of a cash receipt by recognizing revenue, e.g., unearned rent;

    b. reducing an asset, e.g., depreciation, depletion, amortization, including amortization of prepayments and deferrals;

2. assigning manufacturing costs to production departments or cost centers and subsequently to units of product to determine "product cost"; and

3. apportioning the cost of a "lump-sum" or "basket" purchase to individual assets on the basis of their relative market values.

Currently, accountants recognize that within the existing framework of conventional accounting principles and methods, allocations are generally arbitrary. Current allocation theory and practice attempt to allocate portions of the costs of non-monetary inputs in relation to benefits received from them by the enterprise. In this context, benefits involve an increase in the entity's income (or decrease in losses) or are related to cash flows. The generally recognized minimum criteria of any allocation method include the following:

1. The method should be unambiguous.
2. The method should be defendable, i.e., theoretically justifiable.
3. The method should divide up what is available to be allocated, i.e., the allocation should be additive.

The allocation problem in accounting is related to the matching process that assigns the costs of monetary and nonmonetary inputs, such as plant assets and inventories, and revenues, to accounting periods for purposes of determining net income. The objective of this form of allocation is to systematically spread a cost or revenue over two or more time periods. For example, depreciation accounting is a system which allocates the cost of a tangible fixed asset over its estimated useful life.

The allocation of common costs to products or departments is another significant cost allocation problem. Common costs are those costs which are not directly identifiable with a product, process, or department but which result from the joint use of a facility. For example, the cafeteria of a manufacturing plant is used by employees from the manufacturing departments and office department. Some practical way must be found to allocate the cafeteria costs to the various departments (e.g., the number of employees in a department). Common cost allocations are made primarily for product-costing purposes (e.g., inventory valuation). Common cost allocations are frequently arbitrary in nature.

The common cost allocation process involves (1) accumulating costs, (2) identifying the department or process that is to be allocated the costs, and (3) selecting a basis for allocating the common costs to the recipients. Selecting a basis of allocation is often done by examining the past behavior of the cost to determine whether a relation between the costs and an allo-

19

cation base (e.g., number of employees, square footage) can be identified. In some cases, it is possible to evaluate operations to find a logical relation between costs and an allocation base. If these attempts are not productive, then costs would be assigned on an arbitrary base. One method of allocating common costs involves:

1. identifying a number of cost pools associated with administrative and support functions, such as computer center, central stores;

2. arranging these pools from the most general to the most specific;

3. allocating costs from the more general pools are allocated (or stepped down) to the more specific pools, and finally;

4. allocating costs to the primary functions or activities of the organization.

A relatively simple illustration involving two service departments (cafeteria; personnel) and two manufacturing departments (Departments A and B) will illustrate the process:

Cost	Allocation base	Service Cafeteria	Service Personnel	Manufacturing Dept. A	Manufacturing Dept. B	Total
Direct cost	Direct	$ 10,000	$5,000	$50,000	$ 75,000	$140,000
Indirect:						
Rent	Sq. foot	2,000	1,000	10,000	15,000	28,000
Utilities	Sq. foot	4,000	2,000	20,000	30,000	56,000
Totals		$ 16,000	$8,000	$80,000	$120,000	$224,000
Allocation of service depts.:						
Cafeteria	No. of employees	$(16,000)	$2,000	$ 7,000	$ 7,000	—
Personnel	No. of employees		(10,000)	5,000	5,000	—
Totals				$92,000	$132,000	$224,000

Note that costs that can be directly associated with departments are allocated first, e.g., the direct costs. Costs such as rent and utilities are allocated on a rational basis (for example, floor space). Next, service department costs are allocated to manufacturing departments. When service departments service both other service departments and production departments, their costs are usually allocated first. In the illustration, it was decided first to allocate the cafeteria costs to the personnel department and the two manufacturing departments. After a service department's costs have been distributed, no additional costs are allocated to it. The company now knows the costs allocated to the two manufacturing departments. If more than one product comes from the production process, the costs incurred prior to the split-off point of separable products are referred to as *joint costs*. Joint costs are usually allocated to the separable products based on their relative sales value or some physical measure (for example, pounds of beef, board feet of lumber).

The allocation problem also arises when dissimilar assets are acquired for a single lump-sum price. The purchase price must be allocated to the individual assets purchased. The basis for the allocation of the purchase price in lump-sum or "basket" purchases is usually considered to be the relative fair market values of the individual assets. To illustrate a lump-sum acquisition, assume that land and building are acquired for $1,000,000. The fair market values of the land and building are $250,000 and $1,000,000, respectively. The lump-sum purchase price would be allocated to the two assets as follows:

	Appraisal value	Relative fair market value	× Total cost	=	Allocated cost
Land	$ 250,000	$250,000/$1,250,000	× $1,000,000	=	$ 200,000
Building	1,000,000	$1,000,000/$1,250,000	× $1,000,000	=	800,000
	$1,250,000				$1,000,000

A

See also Cost accounting systems; Distribution cost control.

REFERENCE

Thomas, Arthur L., *The Allocation Problem* (American Accounting Association, Evanston, IL, 1969).

B

B

BENEFIT-COST ANALYSIS
Benefit-cost analysis is a procedure or system for evaluating a course of action or program by comparing the costs to the expected benefits from the action or program. If benefits exceed costs, the action or program is considered desirable. The benefit-cost ratio is conceptualized as the present value of the benefits divided by the present value of the costs (or average annual benefits over average annual costs). The analysis is quantified as far as possible; all costs and benefits—direct and indirect, financial, social, and political—are taken into consideration. Difficulties arise when efforts are made to measure intangible costs and benefits, e.g., the benefit of a bypass highway around a city. When benefits cannot be measured, cost-effectiveness evaluations are sometimes used to provide a basis for analysis. Cost-benefit analysis has been widely used

1. to determine whether a particular program, project, or activity is justified;

2. to rank alternative programs, projects, or activities; and

3. to determine the best course of action to attain an objective.

B

Cost-benefit analysis attempts (1) to maximize benefits for a prescribed level of costs, (2) to determine the minimum level of expenditures to achieve some specific level of benefits or objective(s), or (3) to maximize net benefits (benefits minus costs).

The typical benefit-cost evaluation examines the benefits and costs of programs being created or of an existing program. A standard classification for such evaluations is (1) summative evaluations and (2) formative evaluations. Summative evaluations typically seek an answer concerning whether the program works or doesn't work. Answers to such questions as the following are sought: Does the value of the benefits exceed the costs? For alternative programs that accomplish a given task, which is less costly? Such evaluations involving comparative analysis are sometimes referred to as "cost-effectiveness" evaluations. Formative evaluations typically inquire as to whether the program can be improved.

Benefit-cost analysis usually involves the following activities: alternatives are compared; benefits and costs are specified and measured for the current and future periods; the benefit-cost approach is applied using common techniques throughout the entity. Benefits and costs include those which willl flow from the project which must be converted into monetary values.

Cost-benefit analysis is not particularly useful in evaluating programs with widely varying objectives or exceedingly broad scope. It is often difficult or impossible to quantify goals and objectives in sufficient detail to permit benefit-cost analysis to function.

Cost-effectiveness analysis is designed to evaluate effectiveness of goal objective attainment. The objective of cost-effectiveness analysis is primarily to determine the most effective program at different levels of achievement. The most effective program is the one that produces the desired performance level for the minimum cost, or attains the maximum level of effectiveness for a given level of cost.

Benefit-cost analysis is widely used by governmental entities at all levels of operations. Industry has used benefit-cost analysis to evaluate such issues as employee morale, pollution, and safety.

Benefit-cost analysis has occasionally been applied to the auditing and accounting standard-setting processes. As applied to auditing, costs often include audit fees and other costs incurred by the entity being audited. Benefits often relate to the reliability of the financial statements being audited and to the discovery or prevention of fraud. It should be kept in mind that many of the benefits associated with an audit accrue to the general public and often are not measurable, while costs of an audit are usually paid for by a particular entity.

See also Planning function; Control function; Incremental cost analysis; Allocation.

REFERENCE

Gramlich, Edward M., *Benefit-Cost Analysis of Government Programs* (Prentice-Hall, Englewood Cliffs, NJ, 1981).

BREAK-EVEN ANALYSIS

The break-even point is the volume of sales at which total costs equal total revenues. Profits equal zero at the break-even point. It is the lowest volume point as which fixed costs are fully absorbed. A sales volume below the break-even point results in a loss; a volume above the break-even point results in a profit. The margin of safety is the difference between actual or budgeted output and the break-even point. Break-even analysis is a technique for studying the relation between revenue, cost, and profit structures to show the effect on break-even point of changes in revenue and costs.

The formula used to compute the break-even point is as follows:

Sales at break-even point = Variable expenses + Fixed expenses

Fixed expenses are those expenses that tend to remain constant in total within a given period of time and over a wide range of activity (the relevant range) regardless of sales volume. Variable expenses are expenses that tend to remain uniform per unit but which vary in total in direct proportion to changes in the level of activity. Mixed expenses (semivariable) represent a combination of fixed and variable expenses. Mixed expenses increase with volume but not in the same proportion.

To illustrate the computation of the break-even formula, assume the following data:

Sales (60,000 units @ $20 per unit)	$1,200,000
Less: Variable expenses (60,000 units @ $12 per unit)	720,000
Contribution margin	480,000
Less: Fixed expenses	400,000
Net income	$ 80,000

The computation of the break-even point follows where S equals sales at the break-even point; variable expenses are expressed as a percentage of sales:

$$S = (\$720,000/\$1,200,000)\ (S)\ + \$400,000$$
$$S = (.60)\ (S)\ + \$400,000$$
$$.40S = \$400,000$$
$$S = \$1,000,000$$

To verify this computation, consider the following:

Sales at the break-even point	$1,000,000
Less: Variable expenses (60% of sales)	600,000
Contribution margin	400,000
Less: Fixed expenses	400,000
Net income	-0-

Note that variable expenses are 60 percent of sales ($720,000/$1,200,000). With a sales price of $20 per unit, it will take sales of 50,000 units ($1,000,000/$20) to break even. A break-even chart is shown for this problem in Exhibit B-1.

Exhibit B–1
Conventional Break-Even Chart

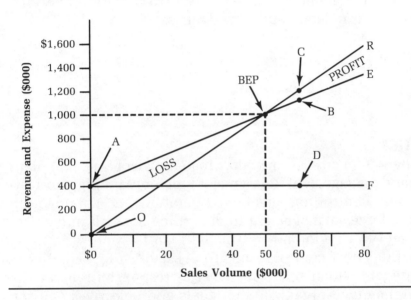

The basic relationship contained in the break-even model can also be used to make additional analyses:

1. changes in sales due to price or volume change,

2. changes in fixed costs due to the level of investment, and

3. changes in variables costs due to price or usage changes.

For example, these relationships should be recognized:

Net income = Sales – Variable expenses – Fixed expenses
or
Sales = Variable expenses + Fixed expenses + Net income

29

B

Using the data in the problem, what sales are required to make a profit of $100,000?

Sales to make = ($720,000/$1,200,000)(S) + $400,00 + $100,000
$100,000 profit

= $1,250,000

See also Contribution margin analysis; Opportunity cost analysis; Incremental cost analysis; Gross margin analysis; Variances; Efficiency and effectiveness.

REFERENCE

Horngren, Charles T., *Introduction to Management Accounting* (Prentice-Hall, Englewood Cliffs, NJ, 1984).

BUDGET

A budget is an orderly and coordinated plan of financial planning and management. It is a major tool for planning, motivating, and controlling business operations. The budgeting process forces management to determine its goals and objectives and to develop a coordinated plan for achieving these ends. Budgetary control results from establishing departmental budgets which relate managerial responsibilities to the requirements of organizational goals and objectives and the continuous comparison of actual with budgeted results to provide a basis for appropriate action.

The master or comprehensive budget is a relatively complete blueprint of the future operations of the firm. The budget period is usually short enough to permit reasonably accurate predictions and long enough to allow time for implementation. The budget period usually coincides with the fiscal period of the business so that actual results of operations can be compared with budgetary estimates. The master budget is usually prepared in terms of (1) an operating budget and (2) a financial budget. The operating budget produces an income statement and supporting schedules. The financial budget consists of a budgeted balance sheet indicating how the budget will affect the company's resources and obligations, including supporting schedules showing cash flow, capital expenditures, and similar items affecting the balance sheet. The operating and financial budgets are usually prepared for a year, with supporting schedules in monthly or quarterly terms. A capital expenditure or project budget is usually developed for a longer time period.

The budgeting process usually involves the determination by a budget committee of basic assumptions under which the details of the budget are to be prepared. The board of directors (or other high-level, decision-making group) approves the assumptions set forth by the budget committee. A budget director then begins to prepare the detailed budget. Detailed budgeting usually begins with a forecast of revenue from sales of products or services. After revenue has been estimated, estimates are made of expenses, costs, collections, and payments. Budgeted financial statements are then compiled and examined to determine how the budgeted activities will affect the company, stockholders, creditors, and other external parties. After this phase of the budgeting process is completed, the budget is implemented.

The second phase of the budgetary control process involves monitoring operations so that operating plans and targets can be attained. Budgetary control relies primarily on analyses of differences (1) between actual costs/revenues and budgeted cost/revenues, and (2) between actual costs and standard costs. Aspects of the control process involve (1) establishing lines of responsibility for performance, (2) communicating plans to those assigned performance responsibilities, (3) evaluating variances between actual results and budgeted estimates, and (4) taking appropriate action thereon.

The master budget which has been discussed here is primarily a planning tool. It is often a static or inflexible budget and is usually prepared for one level of activities—the anticipated or normal level of output. A flexible or variable budget is usually used as the tool for controlling costs and evaluating performance. A flexible budget is prepared for a range of activity because costs are affected by changes in the level of activity. Flexible budgets are often expressed in terms of units of output or in standard direct-labor hours allowed for that output. A simplified flexible budget prepared in terms of product output for three activity levels is shown here:

	Levels of Output Activity		
	10,000	15,000	20,000
Direct materials	$100,000	$150,000	$200,000
Direct labor	50,000	75,000	100,000
Variable factory overhead	20,000	30,000	40,000
Fixed factory overhead	30,000	30,000	30,000
Total costs	$200,000	$285,000	$370,000

If the actual level of output for the period was 15,000 units, actual costs would be compared with the flexible budget prepared at the 15,000 unit level. Any variances between actual costs and budgeted costs should be explained and corrected, if necessary. Performance reports for cost control purposes could be prepared using the following format:

Cost	Actual Costs	Flexible Budget	Variance	Explanation
Supplies	$10,500	$12,000	($1,500)	Special sales

A capital budget is a plan for acquiring and maintaining long-term assets and providing the means of financing these activities. Financial theory strongly supports the separation of the investment decision from the financing decision. A capital budget typically includes one or more of the following:

1. New facilities and major additions.

2. Major renovations and repairs to existing facilities.

A variety of methods are currently used for making investment decisions associated with capital budgeting. The net present value method or some modification thereof is considered the preferred method. The application of the net present value method of capital budgeting involves the following process:

1. Estimate the future cash inflows and outflows for each alternative project under consideration.

2. Discount the future cash flows to the present using the firm's cost of capital.

3. Accept or reject the proposed project according to a decision rule that will maximize the firm's wealth.

Budgeting is considered especially important in governmental accounting. Governmental accounting requires that an annual budget(s) be adopted by every governmental unit. The accounting system should provide the basis for appropriate budgetary control. Budgetary comparisons should be included in the appropriate financial statements and schedules for governmental funds for which an annual budget has been adopted.

Conventional wisdom makes the following assertions concerning budgeting:

1. Planning and budgeting should be integrated. To achieve this end, organizational policies are required, and a philosophy of organizational management must exist.

2. Budgeting is a process for establishing priorities.

3. Planning and budgeting should be data based and outcome (result) oriented.

4. Budgeting is a process of resource allocation. This can give rise to conflicts at and within many organizational levels.

5. Confrontation can result from economic factors (scarcity), allocation processes, lack of understanding, parochialism, and leadership inadequacies.

6. Budgeting is political in nature and involves the arts of persuasion and compromise.

7. There is a permanent dichotomy between organizational needs and wants and the availability of resources.

8. Financial resources are neither inexhaustible nor self-replenishing.

9. Budgeting is a representation in monetary terms of institutional goals and objectives.

10. Budgeting relationships should systematically relate the expenditures of funds to the accomplishment of planned objectives.

11. Budgeting relies on people making optimal choices about economic and noneconomic matters.

12. Budgeting should be adaptive and flexible.

13. Resource reallocation is the main source of flexibility when income growth ends.

14. Judgments and compromises frequently take precedence over computational and bureaucratic forms of decision making.

15. Budgeting decisions are frequently negotiated, often subjectively.

16. Disagreements are often resolved by the use of discretionary power.

See also Comprehensive budget; Cash budget; Capital budget; Planning function; Cost function; Motivation; Communication function; Leadership function; Organizing function; Pricing policy; Goals and objectives; Decision making; Organizational behavior; Performance evaluation.

REFERENCES
Horngren, Charles T., *Introduction to Management Accounting* (Prentice-Hall, Englewood Cliffs, NJ, 1984).
Kaplan, Robert S., *Advanced Management Accounting* (Prentice-Hall, Englewood Cliffs, NJ, 1982).

BUDGETS, TYPES OF
Various types of budgets are used in businesses and not-for-profit institutions. There are five major types of budgets:

1. incremental budget (used with object-of-expenditure, or line-item, budgets),
2. formula budget,
3. planning, programming, and budgeting systems,
4. zero-base budgeting, and
5. performance budgeting.

Incremental budgeting uses an object-of-expenditure approach to budgeting. Incremental budgets show line-item categories of expenditure to be made during the year. Line item refers to objects of expenditures, such as salaries and supplies. In incremental budgeting, either each line item is considered for an increment or it remains unadjusted in the base. Frequently, increments are calculated as uniform percentage adjustments for every line item or group of line items. The basic philosophy is that the current budget is distributed properly among both the functions and objects of expenditures and that little programmatic change needs to occur. Changes in institutional priorities often result through ad hoc determination concerning what increase is needed to effect a programmatic change. When resources become scarce, incremental budgeting tends to perpetuate the existing programs regardless of how ineffective or inefficient they may be. High-cost programs continue to receive high levels of support. The status quo is reinforced and extended. Incremental budgeting emphasizes the short-run and continuity at the possible expense of the long-run goals of the organization. It encourages spending at the risk of jeopardizing cost control efforts.

Formula budgeting is the technique by which the financial needs or operating requirements of an institution may be determined through the application of a formula. Formula budgeting is an objective procedure for estimating the future budgetary requirements of an institution by manipulating data about future programs and by utilizing relationships between program and cost. Formula budgeting is frequently used in not-for-profit institutions, such as colleges and universities.

Planning, programming, and budgeting systems (PPBS) is a managerial technique designed to merge the planning process with the allocation of funds by making it difficult to allocate funds without planning. PPBS emphasize performance, i.e., output and efficiency. The focus of PPBS has also been defined as essentially a planning device that ultimately leads to a conventional department budget for operation and control. PPBS is also described as a macroeconomic, centralized, top-down policy and long-range planning tool. In PPBS, planning involves the selection and identification of long-range objectives of the organization and benefit-cost analysis of various courses of action. Zero-base budgeting demands a total rejustification of every activity from base zero, instead of incrementing the new on the old. The objective of zero-base budgeting is to examine each activity in a manner similar to a proposed new activity to determine whether the activity is necessary. The major focus of zero-base budgeting is on ensuring that managers evaluate their areas of responsibility more completely and more objectively than under other budgeting procedures.

Performance budgeting is a budgeting structure that (1) focuses on activities or functions which produce results and

B

from which resources are used or (2) promotes a budgetary process that attempts to link organizational objectives to resource utilization. Its principal focus is on improving efficiency by means of activity classifications and cost measurements. The common components of most performance budgeting systems are activity classifications, performance measurements, and performance reports. A major problem in implementing performance budgeting has been the difficulty in determining appropriate performance criteria.

Budgets can also be classified as operating budgets and capital budgets. Operating budgets are general-purpose budgets used to formalize activities in relation to financial considerations for a period, usually a fiscal year. They represent short-term planning and control techniques. Capital budgets are budgets representing the expenditures, and the means of financing these expenditures, to be expended for long-lived, or capital, assets, including land, buildings, and equipment.

See also Budget; Comprehensive budget; Capital budget; Benefit-cost analysis.

C

CAPITAL BUDGET

Capital budgeting is a formal process of long-term planning for relatively large, permanent acquisitions and commitments of a firm's economic resources. Long-term investment decisions relate to the following basic areas which have for their objective profit maximization:

1. equipment acquisition and replacement required, e.g., to deal with obsolescence, competition, or legal requirements;

2. cost-saving investments to promote efficiency; and

3. expansion opportunities, e.g., diversification, product lines, and research and development investments.

In evaluating captial budgeting projects, management must consider two major factors:

1. the cost of the investment, and

2. the potential net increase in cash inflows (or reduction in cash outflows) resulting from the proposed investment.

C

Four methods of capital budgeting are widely used in business:

1. the accounting method,
2. the payback method,
3. the net present value method, and
4. the discounted cash flow method.

Accounting method. The accounting method is based on the application of the following equation to evaluate capital projects:

$$\text{Accounting rate of return} = \frac{\text{Expected increase in income}}{\text{Expected increase in investment}}$$

To illustrate the accounting method, assume that management is considering the purchase of a new machine for $11,000. The machine has an expected useful life of five years and a scrap value of $1,000 at the end of this useful life. For the next five years, the machine will create cost savings of $4,000 per year. The accounting rate of return can be calculated this way:

$$\text{Accounting rate of return} = \frac{\$4,000}{(\$11,000 - \$1,000)}$$
$$= 40\%$$

The firm must now decide whether a rate of return of 40 percent is adequate for this project. The accounting rate of return's most serious drawback is that it ignores the time value of money. Expected future dollars are regarded as equal to present dollars.

Payback method. The payback period is the time required for the cash inflow from an investment to accumulate to a total equal to the original cash outlay required for the investment. Using the data from the discussion on the accounting method, the payback period may be calculated as follows:

42

Payback period = Initial investment/Annual cash savings
              = $11,000/$4,000
              = 2.75 years

Management chooses the investment that provides the quickest payoff regardless of which investment may give the highest rate of return over the long run. When using this method, management often sets a maximum payback period for acceptable investments. Investments that exceed the maximum period are rejected. A reasonable payback is usually considered to be between two and five years.

If the inflow of cash savings is not the same from year to year, the payback period may be calculated by adding the cash proceeds in successive years until the total equals the original outlay.

Net present value method. The net present value method uses present values of streams of earnings or costs in evaluating investment decisions. When this method is used, expected future cash inflows and outflows associated with the investment are discounted to the present time, using a minimum discounting rate acceptable to management. The net present value is the difference between the present cost of the investment and the present value of the cash inflow expected from the investment. If the net present value is positive, the investment is acceptable. If the net present value is negative, the investment does not promise to provide a return at a minimum level and should be rejected. Net present value can be conceptualized as follows:

Net present value = present value of net cash inflows
                      − cost of the investment

To illustrate the net present value method, use the data for the machine that cost $11,000, with a scrap value of $1,000 and a useful life of five years. If the company expects a 16 percent minimum rate of return for this type of investment, the

C

machine should not be purchased. The rationale for this decision is given in the illustration shown in Exhibit C-1.

1. Dollar amounts of cash inflows and outflows are recorded in the columns for the appropriate periods.

    a. Direction of each cash inflow is indicated. Cash outflows are negative amounts, and cash inflows or savings are shown as positive amounts.

    b. The timing of each flow is indicated by recording it in the appropriate period.

2. Present value discounting factors are determined from present value tables and entered in the appropriate column (note that the cash operating savings can be treated as an annuity since they are equal each period).

3. Present values of each item are computed and entered in the last column whose figures are then totaled to determine the net present value of the investment.

Exhibit C–1
Worksheet for Net Present Value Problem

	Cash flows at end of period						Discount factor	Total present value
	0	1	2	3	4	5		
Initial cost	$(11,000)						1.000	$(11,000)
Cash operating savings		$4,000	$4,000	$4,000	$4,000	$,4000	3.2741	13,096
Disposal value						1,000	.4761	476
Net present value								$ 2,572

Note: 16 percent discount rate assumed.

Because the net present value of the investment in the machine is positive, the investment in the new machine is considered desirable. The underlying concept for this method is the idea that the company can earn more by buying the machine than it could by putting the same amount of cash into some other investment that earns a 16 percent rate of return. The effect of this decision rule is to accept any proposed investment that offers more than a 16 percent rate of return.

If income taxes are considered, the payment of income taxes represents a cash outflow; a tax savings represents a cash inflow. If we assume a 48 percent income tax rate, each dollar of cash revenue equals only $0.52 after-tax cash inflow while each dollar of cash expense equals only $0.52 after-tax cash outflow. Cash savings on depreciation equals depreciation expense multiplied by the income tax rate. If the problem involving the machine is reworked to take a 48 percent income tax into consideration, the problem would be solved as shown in Exhibit C-2. In this case, the net present value of the investment is negative, so the investment in the machine is rejected.

Exhibit C–2
Net present value method including income tax implications

	Cash flows at end of period						Discount factor	Total present value
	0	1	2	3	4	5		
Initial cost	$(11,000)						1.000	$(11,000)
Cash operating savings		$2,080	$2,080	$2,080	$2,080	$2,080	3.2741	6,810
Disposal value						1,000	.4761	476
Depreciation impact on income taxes		960	960	960	960	960	3.2741	3.143
Net present value								$ (571)

Discounted cash flow method. The discounted cash flow method of capital budgeting finds the discounting rate that results in a net present value of zero for the cash flows. This rate is the expected rate of return on the investment project. The discounting rate can be determined through the use of tables or with a trial-and-error approach. With the discounted cash flow approach. the decision rule takes the following form:

45

if the computed rate of return on the investment exceeds a minimum acceptable rate imposed by management, the investment is considered acceptable. Otherwise, it is rejected.

Using data for the machine purchase provided earlier in this entry and taking income taxes into consideration, the following computations are made:

1. Determine the expected after-tax savings from the investment ($2,080 + $960 = $3,040) per year for five years.

2. Determine the cash outflow for the intial cost of the investment, $11,000.

3. Determine the present value of other cash inflows such as salvage value, $1,000 at the end of five years or $476 now ($1,000 x .476 = $476).

4. Find the discount factor that will equate the expected cash inflows to the present value of the cash outflows:

$$\$3,040 \text{ x Factor} = (\$11,000 - \$476)$$
$$(\$3,040)(\text{Factor}) = \$10,524$$
$$\text{Factor} = 3.4618$$

5. Find the discounting rate that gives a discount factor of 3.4618 for a five-year annuity at an unknown discount rate. This is the discounting rate for which an annuity of $3,040 for five years has a present value of $10,524. Refer to the present value of annuity table to find the discount rate that, for five periods, equals or approximates the computed "factor value." The factor is about 14 percent which is less than the 16 percent minimum rate acceptable to management. The project is rejected.

Capital budgeting projects are frequently complicated when:

1. the amounts to be invested occur over a period of time,

2. the amounts differ, and

3. the timing is irregular.

These problems can usually be dealt with by converting all investments and returns to their discounted total values, at a particular point.

See also Budgets; Comprehensive budget.

REFERENCES

Bierman, Harold, Jr., and Smidt, Seymour, *The Capital Budgeting Decision: Economic Analysis of Investment Projects* (Macmillan, New York, 1980).

Benston, George J., ed., *Contemporary Cost Accounting and Control* (Dickenson, Encino, CA, 1977).

CASH BUDGET

The management of cash is of major importance to most organizations. Cash management involves two problems: (1) the determination of the most desirable balance for the cash account, and (2) the safeguarding of cash. Cash budgeting can deal effectively with both of these problems.

Cash budgeting is one of the most essential parts of a company's planning and control process. The objective of cash budgeting is to project all cash receipts and disbursements with the maximum accuracy and detail, including any arrangements to ensure an adequate supply of cash to meet the needs of the firm.

A cash forecast requires the projection of the plans and estimates of activities that cause cash flows—for example, sales, inventory acquisitions, and operational expenses. The forecast of cash must be coordinated with available information about accounts receivable, investments, accounts payable, etc. These are the steps involved in preparing a cash forecast:

1. Estimate cash receipts for the period. This requires estimates of such items as cash sales of merchandise, collections of receivables, sales of assets, etc.

2. Estimate cash disbursements for the period. This requires estimating cash purchases of merchandise, payments of expenses, repayments of loans, etc.

3. Estimate cash balance at the end of the period. This is done by taking the beginning cash balance, adding estimated cash receipts, and subtracting estimated cash disbursements.

4. Forecast the financing that will be required to maintain a desired minimum cash balance, or forecast the amount of excess cash that will be available for investment or other uses.

5. Prepare the cash budget.

6. Revise and update the cash budget as necessary throughout the year.

Exhibit C-16 illustrates a format that can be used to develop a cash budget.

See also Budget; Comprehensive budget; Cash management.

CASH MANAGEMENT

Cash is a major working capital asset. As a major resource, it should be managed. The objectives of cash management are to keep the amount of cash available to an organization within prescribed limits, to borrow cash at minimum cost, and to invest cash at the maximum return acceptable to the company. Cash management is usually defined as having four major elements: forecasting cash, managing cash flows, investing surplus cash, and maintaining banking relations.

Cash is an unproductive asset; excessive cash retained on hand is undesirable. Insufficient cash creates liquidity and credit problems for the firm.

The preparation of a cash budget is a basic tool of forecasting cash (see entry Cash budget). The cash budget establishes the sources, timing, and amounts of cash receipts and disbursements. Cash budgets can identify the high and low points in a company's cash cycle. Low points alert management not to schedule large discretionary payments during these periods. High points enable management to plan a short-term investment strategy to utilize profitably an excess of funds.

Cash management requires that good internal control procedures be established for cash receipts and cash payments. These cash receipt controls are recommended:

1. All cash receipts should be recorded immediately upon receipt.

2. Total cash receipts should be deposited daily in a bank account.

3. The custody of cash should be entrusted to a person who is not entitled to authorize or record cash transactions.

Cash payment controls recommended to provide internal control over cash disbursements include the following:

1. All disbursements of cash should be made by checks preprinted with sequential numbers.

2. A check should be issued only when the request is supported by evidence relating to the expenditure and is duly authorized. The supporting evidence should be cancelled when the check is written.

3. The person authorized to sign checks should not have the authority to approve check requests or to be involved in recording cash transactions.

4. The bank statement should be periodically reconciled to the company's records by a person not involved either in the receipt or disbursement of cash or in authorizing and recording cash transactions.

5. An internal audit or count of cash on a surprise basis should be conducted at irregular intervals.

6. A fidelity bond should be required for persons who have custody of cash.

7. A cash budget should be used to plan and control the use of cash.

The two objectives of managing cash flows are efficiency and profit. Managing cash flows is performed primarily by:

1. forecasting cash receipts and disbursements (cash flow statement; sales forecasts; surplus/deficiency noted),

2. accelerating cash receipts (bill faster, bill accurately, offer discounts, place invoices with shipped goods, instruct customers to send payments to regional offices),

3. planning and slowing cash disbursements (slow the payment of bills, take advantage of float), and

4. investing excess cash balances (safety/liquidity; return on investment).

See also Budgets; Cash budget; Comprehensive budget; Forecast; Forecasting financial requirements; Working capital.

CENTERS
Organizations typically are organized in terms of responsibility centers, depending upon the type and extent of authority and responsibility assigned to the center. Four major types of centers frequently established by businesses include profit centers, revenue centers, expense centers, and investment centers.

A profit center is a subunit or segment of an organization that is accountable for planning and controlling both revenues and expenses. A profit center is analogous to an independent business, although certain investment and financing activities are sometimes not delegated. Subunits of an organization are frequently organized as expense centers where managers have no control over sales revenue or investment decisions. Expense centers exercise control over costs through the use of standard costs systems and operating budgets.

An investment center can be conceptualized as a profit center that also has planning and controlling responsibilities for investment decisions associated with capital assets. These combined responsibilities make managers of investment centers similar to managers of independent businesses. Long-term financing decisions are frequently reserved to the home office or parent corporation. Managers of such centers are responsible both for the profitability and the return on investment of their centers.

See also Centralization versus decentralization; Organizational behavior; Planning function; Control function; Responsibility accounting.

REFERENCE
Fallon, William K., ed., AMA Management Handbook (AMACON, New York, 1983).

CENTRALIZATION VERSUS DECENTRALIZATION
Organizations can be organized in two ways: centralized or decentralized. From an organizational viewpoint, centralization and decentralization are issues of how authority is delegated to the different organizational levels. Centralization refers to the organizational level that has authority to make a decision. When decisions are delegated to lower organizational levels, the organization is decentralized.

Decentralization gives greater autonomy to to subunits of the organization. In a decentralized firm, decision-making authority is pushed downward through the organizational levels to enable effective planning and activities at the most appropriate level. Decentralized operations enable the firm to fulfill its objectives while providing sufficient autonomy to managers to enable them to test their ideas, skills, and to develop their potential. Communication and coordination are more effective and decisions can be made more quickly in a decentralized organization. In a decentralized organization, the risk exists that managers will promote their decentralized unit at the expense of the company as a whole. The extent to which a firm centralizes its operations depends on the firm's environment (e.g., competitive situation, market characteristics), the size and growth rate of the firm, and the firm's characteristics (e.g., costs and risks involved; top management's preference; available managerial skills; the history of the entity; and benefit-cost considerations). Delegation of authority requires that authority, responsibility, and accountability be co-extensive.

In a centralized organization structure, decision making and coordinating functions are concentrated at the higher levels of the organization structure. Operational activities and responsibilities remain at the lower levels. Centralized operations are usually used by a firm that wants to provide greater uniformity of actions or integration of organizational effort.

See also Control function; Motivation; Performance evaluation; Delegation.

REFERENCE
Fallon, William K., e.d., *AMA Management Handbook* (AMACON, New York, 1983).

COMMUNICATION FUNCTION

Communication is defined as the reporting of pertinent information to management and others for internal and external uses. Communication information that is relevant to the management of an enterprise. Communication is a function of the organizational structure and relationships. Major managerial functions of planning, organizing, directing, and controlling are carried out through communication. Exhibit C-3 shows the major elements of a communication model.

Exhibit C–3
Communication Flows

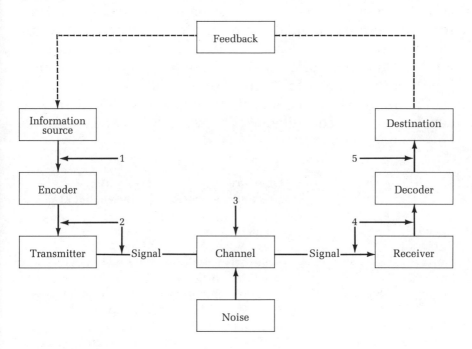

Source: Robert N. Blakeney and Eugene C. Bell, *Advanced Leadership* (Houston, Human Resources Center, College of Business Administration, University of Houston).

Issues associated with communication include:

1. What should be communicated?

2. Who should communicate?

3. When should information be communicated?

4. Where should information be communicated?

5. How should information be communicated?

The human element in communication is affected by cognitive and affective factors. Cognitive factors relate to content and rational thought contained in the message; affective factors relate to values, emotions, and feelings. For communication to be effective, both the cognitive and affective factors must be in harmony. To reduce or eliminate error in communicating, communication models provide for repetition and verification. For example, repetition may involve the use of both written and oral forms of the same message. Verification involves procedures for independent feedback.

Communication models include one-way and two-way communication. The differences between these two models can be summarized as follows:

	One-way (without feedback)	Two-way (with feedback)
Speed	Faster	Slower
Accuracy	Less	More
Noise	Relatively quiet	Relatively noisy
Order	Relatively orderly	Relatively disorderly
Feelings of receiver	Anxiety, insecurity	More confident, less anxious
Feelings of communicator	More confident, secure	Threatened, attacked, less secure

In interpersonal communication, communicating generally is improved if both parties (1) understand that communication has both cognitive and affective components and (2) verify to each other (provide feedback of) their understanding of what the other party means.

In formal communication, the organizational structure of the entity establishes the channels of communication. In informal communications, networking and the grapevine supplement the formal structure provided by the enterprise. In the formal structure, communication occurs in four directions:

downward, upward, horizontally (across boundaries on the same organizational level), and diagonally (across both a horizontal and a vertical boundary). Horizontal and diagonal directions are commonly referred to as cross communication. Some organizational behaviorists maintain that where cross communication is allowed, all parties should obtain advance permission from their superiors and should inform their superiors of any significant developments resulting from the communication. Formal communication systems involve policies (principles or rules of action), standards (for conformity and evaluation), and procedures (detailed instructions, usually provided for in procedural manuals).

Research in organizational communication suggests that:

1. As information flows through an organization, it is frequently translated, altered, filtered, sharpened (highlighted) or leveled (selectivity), and evaluated. These transformations can either facilitate or distort communication.

2. Downward communication is more easily accomplished than is upward communication. Downward communication tends to be unfavorable and important while upward communication tends to be favorable and unimportant.

3. Trust and accuracy are essential in interpersonal and organizational communication. Trust is reflected in the openness and honesty of the communication; accuracy is reflected in the content of the communication. Trust is established by a communicator who is trustworthy (believable, ethical) and informed (experienced, competent).

4. Performance is improved when subordinates are provided with information required to improve performance along with accurate information about their performance.

See also Planning function; Control function; Motivation; Leadership function; Management; Organizational Behavior; Performance evaluation.

REFERENCE
Dessler, Gary, *Organization Theory* (Prentice-Hall, Englewood Cliffs, NJ, 1985).

COMPREHENSIVE BUDGET

The comprehensive budget, sometimes referred to as the master budget, is a complete expression of the planned operations of the firm for a period. The master budget typically has two elements: an operating budget and a financial budget.

The operating budget describes the relationship of the input (efforts) of the firm to final output and sales (accomplishments). The financial budget describes the impact of budgeting on the balance sheet, especially as it relates to economic resources and obligations.

The preparation of a comprehensive budget usually begins with the anticipated volume of sales or services, which is a crucial factor that determines the level of activity for a period. In other cases, factory capacity, the supply of labor, or the availability of raw materials could be the starting point.

A top-down or a bottom-up approach can be used to forecast sales. The top-down approach would first forecast sales based on an examination of the economy, then the company's share of the market and the company's sales, and would proceed to a forecast of sales by products or other category. The bottom-up approach would forecast sales by product or other category, then company sales, and then market share. Both methods should result in sales forecasts of materially the same amount. Quantitative methods of forecasting include (1) historical projections; (2) time series analysis relating to secular trend, cycles, seasonal fluctuations, and random fluctuations using methods such as moving average, exponential smoothing, and time series analysis; and (3) regression analysis. Forecasting methods are discussed in more detail under the entry Forecast.

The sales budget. Two sales budgets are usually prepared— one expressed in units and the other in dollars. In service enterprises, forecasts of revenue from services would be the starting point. The sales budget is developed by accumulating sales projections from the sales department market studies, extrapolation of current sales, or statistical analysis involving such factors as gross national product, disposable personal income, and so on. The sales budget can be categorized according to sales territories, products, sales representatives, regions, customers, and so on. Exhibit C-4 shows the sales budget in units by territories for a company. Exhibit C-5 shows the sales budget in dollars for the firm where the sales price for its product during the coming year is set at $10 per unit.

Exhibit C–4
Sales Budget: Units

Super-Glo, Inc.
Sales budget: units
For the year ended December 31, 1985

Territory	Total	1st Quarter	2nd Quarter	3rd Quarter	4th Quarter
Eastern United States	13,000	2,500	3,000	3,500	4,000
Western United States	5,500	1,000	1,500	2,000	1,000
	18,500	3,500	4,500	5,500	5,000

Exhibit C–5
Sales Budget: Dollars

Super-Glo, Inc.
Sales budget: dollars
For the year ended December 31, 1985

Territory	Total	1st Quarter	2nd Quarter	3rd Quarter	4th Quarter
Eastern United States	$130,000	$25,000	$30,000	$35,000	$40,000
Western United States	55,000	10,000	15,000	20,000	10,000
	$185,000	$35,000	$45,000	$55,000	$50,000

Different approaches are used to forecast sales demand. The most common approaches are (1) market-based (macro) forecasts and (2) sales-based (micro) forecasts. Market-based forecasts usually involve demand curves, economic models, and customer surveys (market research). Sales-based forecasts involve (1) the extrapolation of past sales experience and (2) projections by the company's sales personnel.

Cost-of-goods-sold budget. Based on the estimate of sales volume, the company can prepare an estimate of the cost of the units that can be sold. The company estimates that the cost of the product will be $6 per unit. The cost-of-goods-sold budget is prepared by applying this unit cost to the number of units sold. Exhibit C-6 shows a cost-of-goods-sold budget for the firm.

Exhibit C–6
Cost-of-Goods-Sold Budget

Super-Glo, Inc.
Cost-of-goods-sold budget

Territory	Total	1st Quarter	2nd Quarter	3rd Quarter	4th Quarter
Units (exhibit C-4)	18,500	3,500	4,500	5,500	5,000
Unit cost	6	6	6	6	6
Cost of sales	$111,000	$21,000	$27,000	$33,000	$30,000

Selling expense budget. The selling expense budget present the financial implications of the marketing activity of the firm. Exhibit C-7 shows the selling expense budget for the firm. Exhibit C-8 shows the budgeted cash requirements to meet selling expenses. Depreciation expense is excluded from this schedule because depreciation does not require a cash expenditure.

Exhibit C–7
Selling Expense Budget

Super-Glo, Inc.
Selling expense budget
For the year ended December 31, 1985

	Total	1st Quarter	2nd Quarter	3rd Quarter	4th Quarter
Commissions	$18,500	$3,500	$4,500	$5,500	$5,000
Rent: equipment	4,000	1,000	1,000	1,000	1,000
Advertising	5,000	2,500	500	500	1,500
Telephone	3,000	1,200	400	400	1,000
Depreciation	600	150	150	150	150
Other	10,000	3,000	2,000	2,000	3,000
	$41,100	$11,350	$8,550	$9,550	$11,650

Exhibit C–8
Selling Expense Budget: Cash Requirements

Super-Glo, Inc.
Selling expense budget: cash requirements
For the year ended December 31, 1985

	Total	1st Quarter	2nd Quarter	3rd Quarter	4th Quarter
Total selling expenses	$41,100	$11,350	$8,500	$9,550	$11,650
Less: depreciation expense	600	150	150	150	150
Cash requirements	$40,500	$11,200	$8,400	$9,400	$11,500

C

Administrative expense budget. Most administrative expenses are relatively independent of the predicted sales volume. An administrative expense budget and a budget showing cash requirements for administrative expenses are shown in Exhibits C-9 and C-10, respectively. Bad debts expense is a noncash item and is subtracted from administrative expenses.

Exhibit C–9
Administrative Expense Budget

Super-Glo, Inc.
Administrative expense budget
For the year ended December 31, 1985

Expense	Total	1st Quarter	2nd Quarter	3rd Quarter	4th Quarter
Salaries	$11,900	$3,000	$2,500	$3,000	$3,400
Insurance	1,150	300	400	250	200
Telephone	1,100	400	200	200	300
Supplies	2,700	800	600	600	700
Bad debts expense	1,850	350	450	550	500
Other	1,900	400	500	200	800
	$20,600	$5,250	$4,650	$4,800	$5,900

Exhibit C–10
Administrative Expense Budget: Cash Requirements

Super-Glo, Inc.
Administrative expense budget: cash requirements
For the year ended December 31, 1985

	Total	1st Quarter	2nd Quarter	3rd Quarter	4th Quarter
Administrative expense	$20,600	$5,250	$4,650	$4,800	$5,900
Less: Bad debts expense	1,850	350	450	550	500
	$18,750	$4,900	$4,200	$4,250	$5,400

Budgeted income statement. A budgeted income statement can be developed from the separate budgets which have been prepared. (See Exhibit C-11.) This statement projects the end-of-the-period income and serves as a guide or target for the company. The income statement also makes some additional assumptions:

1. the federal income tax rate is an estimate based on anticipated earnings, and

2. the company can borrow at 12 percent interest.

Exhibit C–11
Budgeted Income Statement

Super-Glo, Inc.
Budgeted income statement
For the year ended December 31, 1985

	Total	1st Quarter	2nd Quarter	3rd Quarter	4th Quarter
Sales (ex. C-5)	$185,000	$35,000	$45,000	$55,000	$50,000
Cost of goods sold (ex. C-6)	111,000	21,000	27,000	33,000	30,000
Gross margin	74,000	14,000	18,000	22,000	20,000
Operating expenses:					
Selling (ex. C-7)	41,100	11,350	8,550	9,550	11,650
Administrative (ex. C-9)	20,600	5,250	4,650	4,800	5,900
Total operating expenses	61,700	16,600	13,200	14,350	17,550
Income from operations	12,300	(2,600)	4,800	7,650	2,450
Interest expense	1,140	420	420	180	120
Income before income taxes	11,160	(3,020)	4,380	7,470	2,330
Income taxes	5,580	0	680	3,735	1,165
Net income	**$5,580**	**$(3,020)**	**$3,700**	**$3,735**	**$1,165**

Accounts receivable collections budget. The accounting department submits data about predicted collections on accounts receivable. From this data, a budget of accounts receivable collections can be prepared (Exhibit C-12). This company makes all of its sales on account, and past experience indicates that 90 percent of sales are collected during the quarter in which the sales are made; 9 percent are collected in the following quarter; the remaining 1 percent are uncollectible. During the first quarter, the company expects to collect $4,000 cash on 1984 credit sales. The information in Exhibit C-12 is computed from the sales budget (Exhibit C-5) and the information about expected collections.

Exhibit C-12
Budget of Accounts Receivable Collections

Super-Glo, Inc.
Budgeted of accounts receivable collections
For the year ended December 31, 1985

On sales made in	Total	1st Quarter	2nd Quarter	3rd Quarter	4th Quarter
4th quarter 1984	$ 4,000	$ 4,000			
1st quarter 1985	34,650*	31,500	$ 3,150		
2nd quarter 1985	44,550		40,500	$ 4,050	
3rd quarter 1985	54,450			49,500	$ 4,950
4th quarter 1985	45,000				45,000
	$182,650	$35,500	$43,650	$53,550	$49,950

*$35,000 estimated sales less 1 percent ($350) estimated uncollectibles.

Purchases budgets. The purchasing department makes plans for obtaining and stocking the necessary merchandise. The purchasing department summarizes its plans in a purchase budget expressed in units (Exhibit C-13) and in costs (Exhibit C-14); purchase requirements equal sales requirements plus the planned ending inventory minus the beginning inventory.

The company plans to have 2,000 units on hand in inventory at the beginning of 1985 and 1,000 units on hand at the end of each quarter.

The payment-on-purchases budget shows the estimated costs of the purchases (Exhibit C-15). The cost of purchases is estimated to be $6 per unit. The company pays 50 percent of its accounts during the quarter in which the purchases are made; it pays the remaining 50 percent during the following quarter. Accounts payable of $2,000 from the previous year are unpaid at the beginning of the year. The company always takes available purchase discounts as a matter of good business policy. Therefore, net purchase costs were used in preparing the $6 per unit cost estimates.

Exhibit C-13
Purchases Budget: Units

Super-Glo, Inc.
Purchases budget: units
For the year ended December 31, 1985

	Total	1st Quarter	2nd Quarter	3rd Quarter	4th Quarter
Sales	18,500	3,500	4,500	5,500	5,000
Add: Ending inventory	1,000	1,000	1,000	1,000	1,000
Total requirements	19,500	4,500	5,500	6,500	6,000
Less: Beginning inventory	2,000	2,000	1,000	1,000	1,000
Purchase requirements	17,500	2,500	4,500	5,500	5,000

Exhibit C-14
Purchases Budget: Costs

Super-Glo, Inc.
Purchases budget: costs
For the year ended December 31, 1985

	Total	1st Quarter	2nd Quarter	3rd Quarter	4th Quarter
Required purchases (ex. C-13)	17,500	2,500	4,500	5,500	5,000
Cost per unit	$6	$6	$6	$6	$6
Required purchases	$105,000	$15,000	$27,000	$33,000	$30,000

Exhibit C–15
Payment-on-Purchases Budget

Super-Glo, Inc.
Payment-on-purchases budget
For the year ended December 31, 1985

On purchases made during	Total	1st Quarter	2nd Quarter	3rd Quarter	4th Quarter
4th quarter 1984	$ 2,000	$2,000			
1st quarter 1985	15,000	7,500	$ 7,500		
2nd quarter 1985	27,000		13,500	$13,500	
3rd quarter 1985	33,000			16,500	$16,500
4th quarter 1985	15,000				15,000
Payment by quarters	$92,000	$9,500	$21,000	$30,000	$31,500

Cash budget. The cash budget is a projection of cash receipts and cash disbursements for the accounting period being budgeted (see Cash budget). The cash budget is prepared from information found in the previous exhibits. Specific exhibits are cross-referenced in the example of the cash budget in Exhibit C-16. The beginning cash balance for the year is $3,000. Dividends of $5,000 are to be paid in the fourth quarter. The company also plans to buy a vacant lot for $25,000 that will be used in future expansion plans. The company will borrow money to acquire the land. The cash budget will reflect the interest requirements related to this loan.

Budgeted balance sheet. A budgeted balance sheet, or financial budget, can now be prepared (Exhibit C-17). The balance sheet for the end of the previous year is combined with the data produced by the transactions reflected in the various budgets to obtain an estimate of the balance for the end of the year.

Once the operating and financial budgets are prepared and approved, they become the major planning and control document for the period. They reflect the company's plan of operations in financial terms. Comprehensive budgets are generally static budgets; that is, they reflect the probable results of operations at the level of activity specified in the budget. If the scale of operations differs from the planned level, a static budget is not particularly effective for controlling operations. In such situations, flexible budgets are required.

Exhibit C–16
Cash Budget

Super-Glo, Inc.
Cash budget
For the year ended December 31, 1985

	Total	1st Quarter	2nd Quarter	3rd Quarter	4th Quarter
Beginning cash balance	$ 3,000	$ 3,000	$ 1,480	$ 2,430	$ 6,415
Cash collections (ex. C-12)	182,650	35,500	43,650	53,550	49,950
Total	185,650	38,500	45,130	55,980	56,365
Cash payments:					
Purchases (ex. C-15)	$92,000	$ 9,500	$21,000	$30,000	$31,500
Selling expense (ex. C-8)	40,500	11,200	8,400	9,400	11,500
Administratative expense (ex. C-10)	18,750	4,900	4,200	4,250	5,400
Federal income taxes (ex. C-11)	5,580		680	3,735	1,165
Dividends	5,000				5,000
Land purchase	25,000	25,000			
Total	186,830	50,600	34,280	47,385	54,565
Cash excess (deficiency)	(1,180)	(12,100)	10,850	8,595	1,800
Financing:					
Borrowing	14,000	14,000			
Repayment	(10,000)		(8,000)	(2,000)	
Interest	(1,140)	(420)	(420)	(180)	(120)
Net	2,800	13,580	(8,420)	(2,180)	(120)
Ending balance	$ 1,680	$ 1,480	$ 2,430	$ 6,415	$ 1,680

65

Exhibit C–17
Budgeted Statement of Financial Position

Super-Glo, Inc.
Budgeted statement of financial position
December 31, 1985

	1985	1984
Assets		
Current assets:		
Cash	$ 1,680	$ 3,000
Accounts receivable	5,000	4,444
Less: allowance for doubtful accounts	(500)	(444)
Merchandise inventory	6,000	12,000
Total current assets	12,180	19,000
Property, plant, and equipment:		
Land	50,000	25,000
Building	20,000	20,000
Less: allowance for depreciation	(17,600)	(17,000)
Total property, plant, and equipment	52,400	28,000
Total assets	$64,580	$47,000
Liabilities and owners' investment		
Current liabilities:		
Accounts payable	$19,000	$ 2,000
Owners' investment:		
Common stock (1,000 shares outstanding)	25,000	25,000
Retained earnings	20,580	20,000
Total owners' investment	45,580	45,000
Total liabilities and owners' investment	$64,580	$47,000

Forecasting is different from budgeting. Forecasts are essentially best estimates of a future event; budgeting begins with forecasts and arrives at a rational figure for budgeted amounts for a period. Forecasts are translated into budgets.

See also Budgets; Cash budget; Forecast; Planning function; Control function; Goals and objectives; Decision making;

Organizational behavior; Performance evaluation; Quantitative methods; Pricing policy; Financial forecast.

REFERENCE
Rayburn, L. Gayle, *Principles of Cost Accounting with Managerial Applications* (Irwin, Homewood, IL, latest edition).

CONSULTING PROCESS
The consultant's role is varied, but generally should consist of helping an organization by providing advice and solving problems. Consultations should result in the company's becoming more competent in solving similar problems in the future without outside assistance.

The consultant can be a listener or a sounding board to assist the client in solving his/her own problems. The consultant can also be viewed as a coach (jointly solving problems) or an intervener who solves problems and takes action directly. Consultant and client should have a clear understanding of what role the consultant is to provide.

While the consulting process used on particular assignments varies, the process typically follows a basic pattern:

1. Summary of the organization's environment, history, goals, and objectives
2. Objective of the consultation:
   a. Problem(s) identified by client
   b. Problem(s) identified by consultant
3. Method and procedures to be used
4. Consultant's expectation from the client (meetings, records, staff)
5. Scheduling/timetable
7. Follow-up
8. Remuneration for engagement

67

The consultant usually presents the report in both written and oral forms. The final report should typically adhere to the agreed upon plan, indicating which problems have been investigated, which recommendations have been made, and what future commitments have been made. Recommendations should be made in specific terms along with detailed descriptions of how they can be carried out. In the concluding interview, the consultant and the client have the opportunity to discuss the engagement, the findings, and the recommendations.

See also Planning function.

CONTRIBUTION MARGIN ANALYSIS

Contribution margin is defined as sales less variable expenses and can be illustrated as follows:

Sales (50,000 units)	$100,000
Less: Variable expenses	60,000
CONTRIBUTION MARGIN	40,000
Less: Fixed expenses	10,000
Net income	$ 30,000
Contribution margin per unit (50,000 units)	$0.80
Contribution margin rate (on sales)	40%

Variable expenses are those expenses that change in direct proportion to the change in volume of sales over the relevant range of business activity. The total variable expense fluctuates as sales volume fluctuates. The variable expense per unit remains constant. Fixed expenses are those expenses that remain constant at any relevant range of volume within the operating capacity of the firm. The total fixed expenses remain constant; the per unit fixed expense varies with change in volume. Contribution is that portion of revenue that is available to cover fixed expenses and produce a profit.

Contribution margin analysis can be applied to pricing, profit planning, management control, break-even analysis, and other planning and control problems. For example, the break-even point of a business can be computed using the contribution margin approach. The break-even point in units can be computed using the following formula:

$$\text{Sales at break-even point in units} = \frac{\text{Fixed expense}}{\text{Contribution margin per unit}}$$

$$= \frac{\$10{,}000}{\$0.80\ (=\$40{,}000/50{,}000\text{ units})}$$

$$= 12{,}500\text{ units}$$

The contribution margin rate is computed as follows: contribution margin divided by sales. Sales at the break-even point in dollars can be computed using the contribution margin rate as follows:

$$\text{Sales at break-even point in dollars} = \frac{\text{Fixed expense}}{\text{Contribution rate}}$$

$$= \frac{\$10{,}000}{0.40\ (=\$40{,}000/\$100{,}000)}$$

$$= \$25{,}000$$

Using data on contribution margin per unit, management can make quick estimates of the impact on net income resulting from changes in sales:

Change in net income = Change in volume × Contribution margin per unit

Change in net income = Change in sales revenue × Contribution margin rate

$$\text{Change in selling price or unit cost required to achieve a desired contribution margin} = \frac{\text{Desired change in total contribution margin}}{\text{Number of units to be sold}}$$

$$\text{Sales required for desired net income} = \frac{\text{Fixed expenses + Desired net income}}{\text{Contribution margin rate}}$$

$$\text{Change in selling price or unit cost required to achieve a desired contribution margin} = \frac{\text{Desired change in total contribution margin}}{\text{Number of units to be sold}}$$

A cost-volume-profit chart (Exhibit C-18) shows the profit or loss potential for an extensive range of volume. At any level of output, the profit or loss is the vertical difference between the sales line and the total cost line. The break-even point is the intersection of sales and total costs. The contribution margin at any level of output is the vertical difference between the sales line and the variable expenses line. The total expenses and variable expenses lines are parallel; the difference between them equals fixed expense.

Contribution margin analysis facilitates other decisions such as the utilization of scarce resources, make-or-buy equipment, sell now or process further, and plant acquisition decisions. To illustrate several applications, assume the following data about a company that can produce and sell three products or any combination thereof. However, the company's production capacity is limited by the number of machine hours available to produce the products.

	Product A	Product B	Product C
Sales price per unit	$12	$15	$18
Variable expense per unit	7	9	10
Contribution margin per unit	5	6	8
Machine hours to produce one unit	5	3	10
Contribution margin per machine hour	$1	$2	$0.80

Exhibit C–18
Contribution-Margin Chart

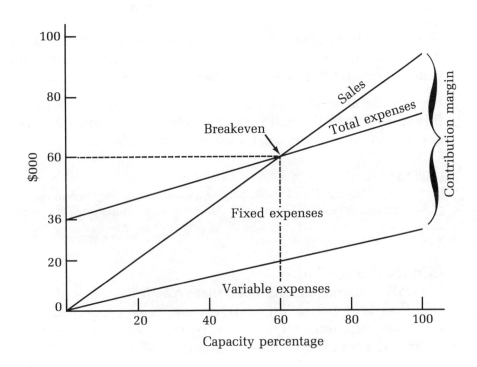

Although Product C has the largest contribution margin per unit, Product B should be produced since it has the largest contribution per the constraining factor (machine hours).

The following illustration shows the income statement for a company that has revenue but is operating at a $20,000 loss. This is considered to be a temporary situation. Should the company continue operations or shut down? If the company closes down, the fixed expenses will continue.

C

	Continue operations	Shut down
Sales	$1,000,000	—
Less: Variable expense	900,000	—
Contribution margin	100,000	—
Less: Fixed expenses	120,000	$120,000
Net loss	$ 20,000	$120,000

The firm should continue to operate because the contribution margin is larger than zero. The contribution margin from continued operations helps pay some of the fixed expenses.

See also Break-even analysis; Gross margin analysis; Planning function; Control function; Cost behavior; Incremental cost analysis; Opportunity cost analysis; Variances.

REFERENCE
Liao, Woody M., and Boockholdt, James L., *Cost Accounting for Managerial Planning, Decision Making and Control* (Dame, Houston, TX, 1985).

CONTROL FUNCTION
Control is a managerial function that provides a degree of assurance that the organization's activities are being performed effectively and efficiently. One of the better-known definitions of control is provided by Henry Fayol:

> *"Control consists of verifying whether everything occurs in conformity with the plan adopted, the instructions issued, and the principles established. It has for an object to point out weaknesses and errors in order to rectify and prevent recurrence."*

The control function consists of setting standards, measuring performance, evaluating results, and taking appropriate action. There is a direct linkage between controlling and planning. Planning provides the institution's goals and objective; control provides one of the means for achieving those goals and objectives. The planning and control cycle is illustrated in Exhibit C-19.

Exhibit C–19
The Strategic Management Process

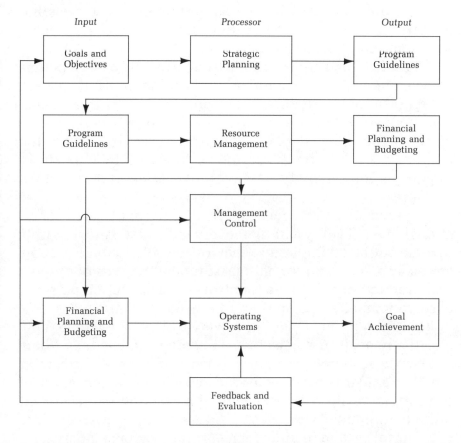

Source: Alan Walter Steiss, *Strategic Management and Organizational Decision Making*, Lexington Books, Lexington, MA, 1985.

Control consists primarily of the acts of:

1. determining that actions undertaken are in accordance with plans, and

2. using feedback to assure that goals and objectives are being attained.

C

Control techniques include both financial and nonfinancial controls. Financial controls focus on monitoring costs, assessing profits or benefits attained, and evaluating asset utilization. Nonfinancial controls monitor important activities and programs as they relate to nonfinancial aspects of efficiency, economy, and effectiveness.

Organizational controls are used to evaluate overall performance, often in terms of profitability, goal attainment, changes in organizational structure, plans, and objectives. Operational controls are used to measure the period-to-period performance by establishing standards which can be used to monitor the performance. Operational controls include such tools and techniques as productivity ratios, unit costs, and workload measures.

Supervisory control relates primarily to control at the operational level. Two generally recognized supervisory controls include output controls and behavior controls. Output controls are usually based on formal measurement records of outputs and productivity. Behavior controls are based upon personal observations of employees and their performance.

Control tells a manager how well a job is being done, how effectively goals and objectives are being achieved, and how efficiently resources are being used. Effectiveness refers to whether a goal is being achieved. Efficiency is a measure of the optimal relationship between inputs (resources used) and outputs (products or services produced). The basic elements of a control system include (1) measurement, or standards; (2) evaluation, or comparisons and feedback; and (3) adjustments or modification.

Control involves five distinct steps:

1. establish performance standards to use for evaluating performance,

2. obtain feedback information on performance,

3. determine whether any modifying action is required under the circumstances,

4. determine what action, if any, is required, and

5. take the necessary action to modify the situation.

Control is accomplished primarily through systems. In a control system design, goals must be integrated with activities that lead to their attainment. Criteria for evaluating control systems are based primarily on three major concerns:

1. how the controls affect human behavior,

2. whether the benefits obtained from the controls exceed the costs of using the control system, and

3. whether the control system's procedures achieve the objectives for which it has been designed.

To be effective, a control system should meet the following criteria:

1. It should be understandable to those doing the controlling and those controlled.

2. It should relate to the organizational structure of the entity controlled.

3. It should relate to the planning process.

4. It should report on a timely basis so that corrective action can be taken.

5. It should provide effective remedial actions.

6. It should communicate corrective action effectively.

7. It should ensure that benefits exceed costs of operating the system.

Controls should be structured around responsibility centers or programs (products, product lines, etc.) within the enterprise. A responsibility center has control over an activity of the organization, such as a department, a division, or a segment of the company. Responsibility centers should be designed so that a particular manager or group has control over an activity for a particular time period. When the responsibility center has control over costs, it is referred to as a cost center. The assembly department of a company would be considered a cost center since the manager of the department would be responsible for costs incurred in the department. If a center has control over both costs and revenues (and therefore profit), it is referred to as a profit center. An investment center is an area of responsibility which has control over revenues, costs, and assets.

Controls commonly used include budgets, performance appraisal, acceptance sampling, program evaluation and review techniques, and variance analysis. The measures used for evaluating performance must relate to the objectives of the responsibility center or program. Control is usually more effective when what is being controlled can be quantified or measured. Quantification of planned data (budgets and standards) and actual data serve as the basic elements of control systems. Variances of actual performance from budgeted performance or standards must be determined and made available to managers on a timely basis if the information derived from the analysis is to be useful.

The information managers ordinarily need to control effectively can be classified as (1) score-card information, (2) attention-directing information, and (3) problem-solving information. Score-card information responds to the question: How well or poorly are we doing? Attention-directing information answers such questions as: Is the company performing according to plans? What problems or opportunities exist? What areas of the enterprise need to be changed, if any? Problem-solving information helps management resolve a particular problem: What is the problem or concern? What are the alternatives? Which alternative is preferable? Reporting and analysis of data developed through a control system is communicated to concerned parties through formal and informal reports.

Controls can be classified in terms of timing: prior, concurrent (or real-time), and post control. Prior controls include those managerial policies, procedures, and activities that contribute to the establishment of a control environment. Concurrent, or real-time, controls are established to identify monitoring signals as an action is being performed so that corrective action can be taken immediately, if required. Post controls take effect after a comparison of actual operations with planned operations. Many quality control systems are based on post controls. Control systems typically follow a defined pattern and timetable period after period.

See also Budgets; Internal control; Planning function; Motivation; Communication function; Leadership function; Organizing function; Management; Management theories; Goals and objectives; Decision making; Organizational behavior; Performance evaluation; Responsibility accounting; Quality control; Distribution cost control; Accounting controls; Administrative controls; Budget; Net-work analysis.

REFERENCE
Woelfel, Charles J., and Mecimore, Charles D., *The Operating Executive's Handbook of Profit Planning Tools and Techniques* (Probus Publishing Co., Chicago, 1986).

CONTROLLER
The controller (or comptroller) is the chief accounting executive in most business organizations. Major functions performed by the controller include internal auditing, general accounting, tax planning, cost accounting, and budgeting. The treasurer is responsible for assuring that the firm has the financial resources required to conduct its activities. In addition, the treasurer usually has responsibilities relating to the custody of cash, banking, investments, and insurance. The treasurer's

C

function is basically custodial; the controller's function is basically information gathering and reporting. The following duties are usually assigned to controllers and treasurers:

Controller:

1. Planning for control
2. Reporting and interpreting reports and statements
3. Evaluating and consulting on financial matters
4. Administering taxes
5. Reporting to government agencies
6. Protecting assets
7. Appraising economic conditions

Treasurer:

1. Providing capital
2. Dealings with investors
3. Financing short-term needs
4. Relating with bank
5. Protecting financial assets
6. Providing for credit and collections
7. Carrying out investments
8. Providing insurance coverage

See also Control function.

COST ACCOUNTING SYSTEMS
Cost accounting is a subset of accounting that develops detailed information about costs as they relate to units of output and to departments, primarily for purposes of providing inventory

valuations (product costing) for financial statements, control, and decision making. Specifically, managerial decisions related to cost accounting include price and output, benefit-cost analysis, capital budgeting, cost estimation, efficiency determination, and performance evaluation. Cost accounting systems are used in both product- and service-oriented organizations as well as in profit and nonprofit organizations.

Manufacturing costs flow through three basic responsibility centers: raw materials storeroom, the factory, and the finished goods storeroom. Three inventory accounts are usually provided to accumulate costs as they relate to the three responsibility centers: raw material inventory, work-in-process inventory, and finished goods inventory. When goods are sold, costs are transferred from the finished goods inventory account to the cost of goods sold account. The flow of costs through the manufacturing process can be illustrated as shown in Exhibit C-20.

Exhibit C–20
Manufacturing Cost Flows

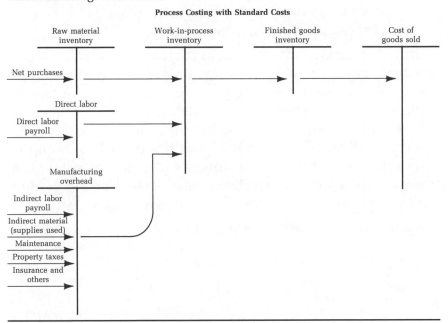

C

A job-order cost system or a process cost system is used to assign costs to manufactured products for purposes of controlling costs and costing products:

1. A job-order (or production order) cost system accumulates costs of material, labor, and manufacturing overhead by specific orders, jobs, batches, or lots. Job-order cost systems are widely used in the construction, furniture, aircraft, printing, and similar industries where the costs of a specific job depend on the particular order specifications.

2. A process cost system accumulates costs by processes or departments over a period of time. Product cost systems are used by firms that manufacture products through continuous-flow systems or on a mass-production basis. Industries that use process cost systems include chemical, petroleum products, textiles, cement, glass, mining, and others. In a process cost system, costs for a department or process are accumulated. Per-unit costs are obtained by dividing the total departmental costs by the quantity produced during a given period in the department or process.

Direct material and direct labor costs can usually be traced directly to particular units manufactured. Manufacturing overhead costs incurred during a period are usually allocated to units manufactured based on a predetermined overhead rate. This overhead rate is based on the budgeted overhead costs for the period and the estimated level of activity (for example, units produced, direct labor hours, direct labor costs). The predetermined factory overhead rate per direct labor hour would be computed as follows, using assumed data:

$$\text{Predetermined overhead rate} = \frac{\text{Estimated overhead costs for the year}}{\text{Estimated direct labor hours for the year}}$$

$$= \frac{\$500,000}{100,000}$$

$$= \$5 \text{ per direct labor hour}$$

If 400 direct labor hours were worked on a particular job, $2,000 overhead costs would be assigned to that job. Any difference between the total overhead costs actually incurred during a year and the total amount assigned to units in production can be charged to cost of goods sold for the year if the amount is not material. If material, the variance can be distributed among the work in process inventory, finished goods inventory, and cost of goods sold.

Standard cost systems are widely used for budgeting and performance evaluation purposes. Standard costs can be used in both job-order and process cost systems. In a standard cost system, product costing is achieved by using predetermined standard costs for material, direct labor, and overhead. Standard costs are developed on the basis of historical cost data adjusted for expected changes in the product, production technology, engineering estimates, and other procedures. Standards may be established at any one of the following levels:

1. Ideal standards are set for the level of maximum efficiency.

2. Normal standards are set to reflect the conditions that are expected to exist over a period of time sufficient to take into consideration seasonal and cyclical fluctuations.

3. Currently attainable standards are set at a level which represents anticipated conditions assuming efficient operations.

Because predetermined standards usually differ from actual costs incurred, a variance typically exists. An unfavorable variance results when actual cost exceeds standard cost; a favorable variance results when standard cost exceeds actual cost. The usual approach followed in standard cost analysis is to separate price factors from efficiency factors. When the actual amount paid differs from the standard amount, the variance is referred to as a price, rate, or spending variance. When the

C

actual input quantity (e.g., ton, labor hours) differs from the standard input quantity, the variance is referred to as a quantity, volume, or yield variance. The relationships between actual and standard price/quantity are illustrated in the following diagram. The diagram shows two types of prices and quantities: actual and standard. A price variance is conceptualized as the difference between quadrants 1 and 2. A quantity variance is reflected in the difference between quadrants 2 and 4.

	Actual Price	**Standard Price**
Actual Quantity	Actual quantity at actual price	Actual quantity at standard price
	Quadrant 1	Quadrant 2
Standard Quantity	Standard quantity at actual price	Standard quantity at standard price
	Quadrant 3	Quadrant 4

The formulas for typical direct material and direct labor variances include the following:

1. Direct material price variance = Actual quantities purchased × (Actual price – Standard price).

2. Material quantity (usage, efficiency) variance = (Actual quantity used – Standard quantity allowed) × Standard price.

3. Direct labor rate variance = Actual hours used × (Actual labor rate – Standard labor rate).

4. Direct labor efficiency variance = (Actual hours used – Standard hours allowed) × Standard labor rate.

82

The following data will be used to illustrate the computation of the direct material and direct labor variances:

Direct material:
  Purchased   10,000 pounds @ $10 per pound
  Standard price $9 per pound
Direct labor
  Purchased   12,000 hours @ $6 per hour
  Standard rate $7

The computations are as follows:

1. Direct materials price variance
   = 10,000 × ($10 - $9)
   = $10,000 unfavorable price variance

2. Direct materials quantity variance
   = $9 × (10,000 pounds - 12,000)
   = $18,000 favorable quantity variance

3. Direct labor rate variance
   = 12,000 × ($6 - $7)
   = $12,000 favorable rate variance

4. Direct labor efficiency variance
   = $7 × (12,000 - 14,000 hours)
   = $14,000 favorable efficiency variance

Controlling overhead costs is usually more difficult than controlling direct material and direct labor costs because it is difficult to assign responsibility for overhead costs incurred. A general approach to controlling overhead costs involves computing two variances: the controllable overhead variance and the overhead volume variance. The controllable overhead variance is the difference between the actual overhead costs incurred and the factory overhead budgeted for the level of production achieved. This variance measures the difference between the overhead costs actually incurred and the costs that should have been incurred at the level of output attained. The

C

overhead volume (or usage) variance is the difference between the factory overhead budgeted for the level of production achieved and the overhead applied to production using the standard overhead rate. A volume variance arises if more or less plant capacity than normal is actually utilized. When the expected capacity usage is exceeded, the overhead volume variance is favorable.

Variances should be analyzed if the cost of doing so does not exceed the benefits that can be expected from the analysis. If the variances are to be analyzed, they should be examined to find their causes. At this point, it should be determined what action should be taken, if any.

Cost accounting systems have been criticized for many reasons. In recent years, critics have mentioned that the reports issued to operating managers are too complex and untimely to reduce costs and improve productivity. Many costs are distributed to products unrealistically, especially those systems which use direct-labor based methods for making the distribution. This can lead to erroneous decisions of product pricing, product mix, and market response to competitors. Cost accounting systems frequently focus on short-term profit cycles, usually monthly, at the expense of long-term goals and objectives of the organization. A short-term emphasis can lead to decreases in investments, research and development, and other long-term opportunities.

See also Costs; Budgets; Planning function; Control function.

REFERENCES

Horngren, Charles T., *Cost Accounting: A Managerial Emphasis* (Prentice-Hall, Englewood Cliffs, NJ, 1981).

Johnson, H. Thomas, and Kaplan, Robert S., *Relevance Lost: The Rise and Fall of Management Accounting* (Harvard Business School Press, Boston, MA, 1986).

COST BEHAVIOR

How costs react to changes in activity (volume) is referred to as cost behavior. Different types of costs behave differently in response to different activity levels and within a relevant range. In the short run, costs are of three types: fixed costs, variable costs, and mixed, or semivariable, costs.

Fixed costs are those costs that remain constant at any relevant range of volume within the existing operating capacity of the firm. The term *fixed cost* relates to total dollar cost. For example, the rent expense of a firm is assumed to be $100,000 for the year. If 1,000 or 10,000 items are manufactured, rent expense remains fixed at $100,000. Note that per unit fixed cost for rent varies inversely with volume because the cost is spread over more units. Rent expense per unit is $100; if 10,000 units are produced, rent expense per unit is $10 per unit.

Variable costs are those costs that change in direct proportion to the change in volume of sales over the relevant range of business activity. The total variable expense fluctuates as the volume fluctuates. The term *variable cost* refers to the variability of the total dollar cost. Assume that a company sells a magazine for $2 per issue. Commission expense is $1 per issue. If 1,000 units are sold, the total sales commission is $1,000; if 10,000 units are sold, the total sales commission is $20,000.

Mixed costs are those costs that contain both a fixed and a variable element. Mixed costs change with increases or decreases in volume but do not change in direct proportion to the volume changes. Telephone expense, maintenance and repair expense, and utilities are usually mixed expenses. If volume should drop to zero, these costs would probably decrease somewhat, but they would not decrease proportionately with the decrease in volume.

Fixed and variable costs are illustrated in Exhibit C-21.

See also Costs; Budget; Fixed and flexible budget.

Exhibit C–21
Variable and Fixed Costs Behavior

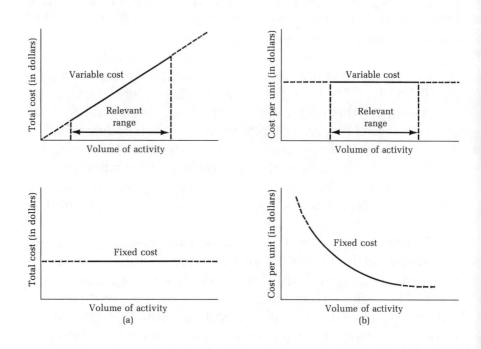

COST OF CAPITAL

The cost of capital usually refers to the cost of funds invested in an enterprise. In this sense, the cost of capital is the weighted average of the cost of each type of debt and equity capital. The weight for each type of capital is the ratio of the market value of the securities representing that particular source of capital to the market value of all securities issued by the company. To illustrate, assume that the market value of a company's common stock is $600,000 and the dividend yield is 10 percent. The market value of the company's interest-bearing debt is

$400,000 with an average after-tax yield of 8 percent. The average cost of capital for the company can be estimated as follows:

Source	Proportion of total capital		Cost		
Common stock	0.60	×	0.10	=	0.06
Debt	0.40	×	0.08	=	0.032
Average cost of capital					0.092

Cost of capital also refers to the discount rate that equates the expected present value of future cash flows to common shareholders with the market value of the common stock at a specific time.

See also Costs; Capital budget.

REFERENCE
Bierman, Harold, Jr., and Smidt, Seymour, *The Capital Budgeting Decision: Economic Analysis of Investment Projects* (Macmillan, New York, 1980).

COSTS

A cost is an expenditure (a decrease in assets or an increase in liabilities) made to obtain an economic benefit, usually resources that can produce revenue. A cost can also be defined as the sacrifice to acquire a good or service, or the effort required to accomplish some goal, objective, or purpose. Used in this sense, a cost represents an asset. An expense is a cost that has been utilized by the company in the process of obtaining revenues; i.e., the benefits associated with the good or service have expired. Costs can be classified in many ways including the following:

1. *Direct and indirect costs:*

   a. Direct costs are outlays that can be identified with a

C

specific product, department, or activity. For example, the costs of material and labor that are identifiable with a particular physical product are direct costs for the product.

b. Indirect costs are those outlays that cannot be identified with a specific product, department, or activity. Taxes, insurance, and telephone expense are common examples of indirect costs.

2. *Product and period costs:*

a. Product costs are outlays that can be associated with production. For example, the direct costs of materials and labor used in the production of an item are product costs.

b. Period costs are expenditures that are not directly associated with production but with a time period. The president's salary, advertising expense, interest, and rent expense are examples of period costs.

3. *Fixed, variable, and mixed costs:*

a. Fixed costs are costs that remain constant in total (not per unit), regardless of the volume of production or sales, over a relevant range of production or sales. Rent and depreciation are typically fixed costs. Total depreciation remains constant; depreciation per unit of output changes with changes in volume or activity.

b. Variable costs are costs that fluctuate in total (not per unit) as the volume of production or sales fluctuates. Direct labor and direct material costs used in production and sales commissions are examples of variable costs. Total commission expense varies with changes in sales volume; commission expense per unit of sales remains constant as sales volume changes.

c. Mixed costs are costs that fluctuate with production or sales, but not in direct proportion to production or sales. Mixed costs contain elements of fixed and variable costs. Costs of supervision and inspections are often mixed costs.

4. *Controllable and uncontrollable costs:*

   a. Controllable costs are costs that are identified as a responsibility of an individual or department, and that can be regulated within a given period of time. Office supplies would ordinarily be considered a controllable cost for an office manager.

   b. Uncontrollable costs are those costs that cannot be regulated by an individual or department within a given period of time. For example, rent expense is uncontrollable by the factory foreman. In theory, all costs are controllable by someone within an organization over an extended period of time.

5. *Out-of-pocket costs and sunk costs:*

   a. Out-of-pocket costs are costs that require the use of current economic resources. Taxes and insurance are generally out-of-pocket costs.

   b. Sunk costs are outlays or commitments that have already been incurred. The cost of equipment already purchased is a sunk cost.

6. *Incremental, opportunity, and imputed costs:*

   a. Incremental (or differential) cost is the difference in total costs between alternatives. Incremental costs can also be considered as the total cost added or subtracted by switching from one level or plan of activity to another.

   b. Opportunity cost is the maximum alternative benefit that could be obtained if economic resources were applied to an alternative use.

   c. Imputed costs are costs that can be associated with an economic event when no exchange transaction has occurred. For example, if a company "rents to itself" a building that it might otherwise have rented to an outside party, the rent for the building is an imputed cost. An implicit cost, such as implicit interest, is a cost implied in a contract.

7. *Relevant cost.* A relevant cost is an expected future cost and a cost that represents difference in costs among alternatives. Assume you purchased an airline ticket from New York to London at a cost of $300 and that you have made an unrefundable $75 downpayment on the ticket. The remaining $225 will be paid when you pick up the ticket. The ticket is nontransferable. You later discover that you can purchase a ticket to London on another airline for $200. Everything related to the two tickets is equal. The $75 downpayment is not relevant to this decision since it is not a future cost that differs among alternatives. You should buy the new ticket for $200.

8. *Discretionary, committed, and recurring costs:*

   a. Discretionary, or managed, costs include costs that can be incurred based on the judgment of management.

   b. Committed costs are usually the result of long-term decisions related to projects, programs, or activities.

   c. Recurring costs are primarily operating costs that vary with the size and duration of a project, program, or activity.

Costs can also be summarized or categorized in a variety of ways. Another meaningful way to classify costs is:

1. by function, e.g., manufacturing costs, selling expenses, general and administrative expenses, direct operating expenses, etc.;

2. by organizational unit, e.g., manufacturing department, shipping department, president's office; or

3. by product or service, i.e., the output of the organization or that which is sold to customers or clients.

Costs can also be classified as follows:

1. On a basis of time.
   a. Historical costs, i.e., when incurred.
   b. Current costs, i.e., fair market value at the current date.
   c. Budgeted cost, i.e., predetermined costs.
2. As behavior in relation to activity (variable, fixed, and mixed costs).
3. By management function (manufacturing, selling, general, and administrative costs).
4. By traceability (direct and indirect costs).
5. As charges against revenue (product and period costs).
6. As decision-making costs (not usually used for recording purposes):
   a. Out-of-pocket vs. sunk costs
   b. Avoidable vs. unavoidable costs
   c. Relevant vs. irrelevant costs
   d. Opportunity costs
   e. Controllable vs. noncontrollable costs
   f. Marginal and incremental (or differential) costs
   g. Variable, fixed, and mixed costs
   h. Imputed and implicit costs

Functional cost categories are a natural way to gather costs and can serve as a basis for controlling costs. Management uses cost classification by organizational units for control purposes and for developing product costs. When classified by organizational units, costs are assigned to areas of responsibility which are subject to control. Product costs are usually required for pricing decisions and profitability evaluations. The product cost classification is useful to establish a value on inventories or cost of goods sold.

See also Cost behavior; Fixed and flexible budgets; Break-even analysis; Contribution margin analysis; Pricing policy; Variances; Cost accounting systems; Incremental cost analysis; Opportunity cost analysis; Cost of capital; Direct costing and absorption costing; Cost behavior; Expenses; Imputed and implicit costs.

REFERENCE
Moscove, Stephen A., et al., *Cost Accounting* (Houghton Mifflin, Boston, 1985).

D

DECISION MAKING

One of the most important characteristics of a business executive is his/her ability to make appropriate decisions. A decision is an action. The result of a decision is that one course of action is taken instead of an alternative course. Decision making is essentially problem solving:

1. what is the problem or concern?

2. what are the alternatives? and

3. which alternative is preferable?

Major factors associated with decision making include:

1. quantitative data, and

2. analysis of quantitative data: systematic method(s) of organizing, summarizing, and analyzing facts.

Decision models are frequently used in making business decisions. Decision models provide some assurance that alternatives are evaluated logically as related to specific criteria and assumptions. Modeling is generally economical in terms of time and effort, is readily understood by the decision maker and decision user, and can be modified as circumstances dictate.

Probability can be used to measure the degree of the likelihood of a particular event occurring. Estimates of probability may be (1) subjective, based on personal estimates of the decision maker, or (2) objective, based on historical experience or logical processes. The decisions typically faced in the business world can be classified as follows:

1. Decisions under certainty (all facts are known); decisions under uncertainty (where the event that will occur— the state of nature) is not known with certainty but probabilities can be assigned to the possible occurrences (the process is stochastic). Decision making under uncertainty typically requires that judgments be made about future events to which outcomes are more likely than others (probability distribution about possible outcomes) and correlates this knowledge with the consequences associated with specific decisions.

2. Decisions where the opponent is nature or a rational opponent.

3. Decisions by an individual or by a group.

When mathematical models are used to solve the decisions described in the preceding paragraph, the following general process can be used:

1. Establish the criterion to be used, the decision rule.

2. Select the model to use and the values of the parameters of the process.

3. Determine the decision which optimizes the criterion.

Decision rules under uncertainty where the decision maker must choose a course of action without knowing the probabilities for the occurrences of the various states of nature include:

1. Maximin rule: maximize the minimum profit of the various alternatives or, if costs (losses) are involved, minimize the maximum cost.

2. Maximax rule: maximize the maximum (where a large gain is considered attractive).

3. Minimax regret rule: minimize the maximum regret.

Decision-making rules when the probabilities of the states of nature are available include the following:

The payoff from a particular action is weighted with the probabilities of each state of nature; the resulting expected payoffs for each action are compared and the strategy with the highest expected payoff is selected.

When the expected average monetary payoff is not considered applicable, a decision maker may judge that a particular decision is preferable to another based on a personal utility function (choices that an individual would make under different circumstances).

Decision trees are useful for analyzing a series of decisions and for clarifying complex situations. Various stages of the decision-making process are shown graphically as separate branches of a decision tree. The decision maker would evaluate the expected payoffs at the far right side of the tree and work back (leftward) to a decision. This process provides the expected value of making a specific decision; this expected value can be used to work backward to evaluate the payoff from the initial decision. A partial decision tree is shown in Exhibit D-1.

Exhibit D–1
Decision Tree for a Project

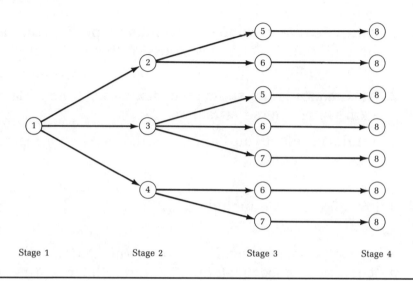

| Stage 1 | Stage 2 | Stage 3 | Stage 4 |

Errors in decision making typically are those which (1) represent a mistake in logic in reasoning from premises to conclusions, or (2) involve the selection of the wrong variables or not enough variables.

General rules for noninvestment decisions where the flow of benefits and costs is even include:

Decision factors	Decision rule
Revenues only	Maximize revenue
Variable costs only	Minimize costs
Costs and benefits within relevant range and below capacity	Maximize contribution margin
Costs and benefits within relevant range and at capacity	Maximize unit contribution per unit of constraining factor

General rules for noninvestment decisions where the flow of benefits and costs is uneven:

1. Maximize the net present value of net after-tax benefits.
2. If there are no net benefits, minimize the net present value of after-tax costs.

Special approaches to business decision making discussed in this book include:

Situation	Encyclopedia entry
1. Cost-volume-profit relationships	Break-even analysis
2. Alternative course of action	Incremental cost analysis Opportunity cost analysis
3. Profitability	Contribution margin analysis
	Gross margin analysis
4. Investment analysis	Return on investment
5. Short-term planning and control	Budgeting
6. Long-term capital projects	Capital budgeting
7. Inventory order point	Inventory model

See also Planning function; Control function; Pricing policy; Management theories; Goals and objectives; Organizational behavior; Performance evaluation; Budget; Forecast; Net-work analysis.

REFERENCES
Baker, Kenneth R., and Kropp, Dean H., *Management Science* (John Wiley & Sons, New York, 1985).
Buffa, Elwood S., *Modern Production/Operations Management* (John Wily & Sons, New York, 1983).

DELEGATION
The delegation of authority and responsibilities is an essential part of the organizing process. Delegation is the primary mechanism for establishing organizational relationships. Delegation assigns managerial and operational functions to specific individuals.

Organizational authorities have identified various aspects of delegation:

1. assigning responsibilities;

2. granting authority commensurate with the assigned responsibilities, including making commitments, using resources, and performing similar managerial duties;

3. establishing an obligation for effective and efficient performance; and

4. providing for feedback and evaluation of performance.

See also Organizational behavior; Centralization versus decentralization; Management theories.

REFERENCE
Daft, Richard L., *Organization Theory and Design* (West, St. Paul, MN, 1983).

DIRECT COSTING AND ABSORPTION COSTING
Direct (or variable) costing and absorption costing are two approaches to product costing. With direct costing, ending inventory includes only variable production costs, such as direct materials, direct labor, and variable manufacturing overhead. Fixed overhead costs, which do not change with changes in production levels (such as rent and insurance), are expensed when incurred. Direct costing theory is based on the assumption that fixed costs (the cost of being in business) are incurred whether or not anything is produced; therefore, variable costs (the cost of doing business) are the true costs of production.

Under absorption, or full or conventional, costing, both fixed and variable production costs are charged to production. With absorption costing, the cost of inventory includes both variable and fixed factory overhead costs. Variable costing is frequently used for decision-making purposes but is not generally accepted for external financial reporting. The differences between the two methods are due entirely to the treatment of fixed factory overhead.

To illustrate the difference between direct and absorption costing, assume the following data. A company that manufactures radios incurred the following costs for the year: raw material costs, $100,000; direct labor costs, $200,000; variable factory overhead, $50,000; fixed factory overhead, $25,000. There were no beginning or ending work in process inventories.

	Direct Costing	Absorption Costing
Direct materials	$100,000	$100,000
Direct labor	200,000	200,000
Variable factory overhead	50,000	50,000
Fixed factory overhead		25,000
Ending finished goods inventory	$350,000	$375,000

When production exceeds sales, absorption costing will cause net income to exceed net income under direct costing because some fixed overhead costs are deferred in inventory rather than being written off as period costs. When sales exceed production, the opposite effects on net income occur because some previously deferred fixed factory costs are included with current fixed overhead costs in cost of goods sold.

Direct costing is useful for controlling current costs and for profit planning (sales promotions; special pricing; make or buy decisions). When direct costing is used, periodic net income varies directly with sales volume since variable costs are proportional to sales. When absorption costing is used, the

D

volume/profit relationship becomes more difficult to estimate since fixed costs are a component of inventory.

See also Costs; Cost behavior; Decision making; Pricing policy: direct cost pricing; Pricing policy: variable cost pricing.

REFERENCES
Morse, Wayne J., *Cost Accounting* (Addison-Wesley, Reading, MA, 1978).
Brock, Horance, and Palmer, Charles, *Cost Accounting Principles and Applications* (McGraw-Hill, New York, 1984).

DIRECTING

Directing is a management function that involves guiding and supervising subordinates in order to achieve goals and objectives of the enterprise. Directing can be justified in relation to what an organization does (its purpose), what it accomplishes (results), how it accomplishes what it does, and why it does what it does (motivation).

The basic ingredients of directing are motivation and leadership. Content and process theories of motivating people have been suggested. Content theories describe the needs that motivate people: incentive payments, human relations (group approval and personal satisfaction), the hierarchy of needs (physiological, security, social, ego needs, self-actualization, and Theory X and Theory Y. Process theories of motivation describe how needs motivate people. Process theories generally fall into one of three groups:

1. expectancy theory: the expectation that effort will be rewarded;

2. equity theory: how outcomes measure up against inputs; or

3. positive reinforcement: behavior is the result of conditioning.

See also Planning function; Control function; Motivation; Leadership function; Performance evaluation.

REFERENCE
Fallon, William K., ed., *AMA Management Handbook* (AMACOM, New York, 1983).

DISTRIBUTION COST CONTROL

The marketing function includes all activities involved in the flow of goods from the point of production to consumption. Distribution, or marketing, costs include such costs as promotion, advertising, transportation, insurance of goods transported, selling expenses, and others. A company attempts to control marketing costs to increase profits, to better control marketing costs, and to justify a company's actions before regulatory bodies which are concerned with marketing policies.

Cost control tools available for controlling marketing operations are usually budgets and standards. Cost controls measure the actual performance of a function against a predetermined standard and investigate any differences between actual performance and standard performance. Cost analysis refers to searching for better ways of performing marketing tasks.

Marketing costs are usually classified as order-getting and order-filling costs. Order-getting costs are costs incurred by direct selling, advertising, and sales promotion functions for the purpose of persuading customers to purchase a product or service. Order-filling costs are marketing costs incurred to perform the sale and include such costs as handling, transportation, and credit and collection functions. Order-filling costs are usually repetitive in contrast with order-getting costs. Order-filling costs tend to vary with sales volume; e.g., warehousing costs normally increase as the number of shipments increase.

Most enterprises keep accounting records which express costs by nature or object of expenditure—for example, wages, rent, insurance—for product line, territory, customers, distribution channel. This classification is sometimes referred to as the natural expense classification which describes the kind of service the company obtained for the expenditures. For analysis purposes, the natural expense item must be distributed to functions, such as credit and collections, transportation, or sales promotion. Certain of these costs are directly related to the function and require no allocation. Other costs are indirect costs which must be distributed to the functions on some rational basis. This requires the allocation of costs to functional areas.

To allocate marketing costs to functions, the factor which causes the marketing costs to vary must be identified. Whatever unit of variability is adopted, the results should be reasonably accurate and economical in application. For example, unit costs for advertising and sales promotion can be determined by using the following units of variability:

Function	Unit of variability
Direct media costs:	
Newspaper	Newspaper inches or gross sales
Radio and television	Minute of radio/television time
Direct mail	Number of items mailed
Sales distributed	Number of samples distributed
Total sales promotion	Sales transactions or units sold
Personnel expense	Number of employees
Filing	Number of units filed
Credit investigation	Credit sales transactions
Mail handling	Number of pieces

If variance analysis is to be used, the variance between actual and standard costs should be explained in terms of price and efficiency variances. These variances are computed as follows:

Price variance = (Standard price – Actual price) × Actual work units
Efficiency, or quantity, variance = (Budgeted work units – Actual work units) × Standard price

Marketing costs are usually budgeted on the basis of:

1. A given amount which is thought adequate to meet expected demand for service;

2. Percentage of expected unit sales;

3. A variable (flexible) budget is used based on a fixed amount per period plus a variable amount per unit sold; or

4. Standard costs multiplied by estimated number of measures.

Short-term profit measures of marketing performance include:

1. budgeted sales and gross margin versus actual,

2. marginal contribution analytical techniques,

3. sales (dollars or physical units),

4. return on assets, and

5. net income.

General and administrative costs are incurred to facilitate both the production and marketing functions. Such costs include management salaries, financial accounting, clerical costs, rent, legal fees, telephone, and other costs. General and administrative costs can usually be controlled through budgeting and standards in a manner similar to that demonstrated for marketing costs.

See also Costs; Control function; Planning function; Allocation; Variances; Efficiency and effectiveness.

E

EFFICIENCY AND EFFECTIVENESS

Effectiveness refers to how a job is performed, i.e., doing things right: does it produce the intended results? Effectiveness of an organization is evaluated in terms of how what is done relates to goals and objectives, i.e., doing the right thing. Efficiency is the relationship of outputs per unit of input. Efficiency relates to an activity performed with the lowest consumption of resources.

Efficiency is related to productivity. Workload, or output, measures refer to the volume of goods or services produced or delivered; unit cost, or input, measures show the resources used to operate a program or activity. When output measures are related to input measures, the result is a performance measure.

Increased productivity is the result primarily of the division of labor and the intensive use of capital. Productivity measures are a subset of performance measures that deal directly with the production process. Productivity can be measured in terms of the relationship between the (1) total units of output and the total units of input of all factors of production used or (2) only one factor of production, e.g., labor cost, capital, or materials:

$$\boxed{\text{E}}$$

(1) productivity = $\dfrac{\text{Units of output}}{\text{Factors of production}}$

(2) productivity = $\dfrac{\text{Units of output}}{\text{Labor costs}}$

Productivity models are available to make the computations. Work measurement and time and motion studies are sometimes used to measure productivity.

A firm can change its cost per unit of output by improving production techniques, by spreading fixed cost over a greater range of output, and by other methods. Production costs are influenced by relationships between factor-of-production inputs and product outputs. This relationship reflects the production function of the firm. The production function describes the way in which costs vary with output.

The optimum proportion of the factors of production is determined by the law of diminishing returns, or diminishing productivity. This economic law states that

> ...as additional units of a factor of production are combined with fixed quantities of other factors, a point will be reached where the increase in output resulting from the use of an additional unit of that factor will not be as large as was the increase in output due to the addition of the preceding unit. Exhibit E-1 illustrates the law of diminishing returns as reflected in productivity curves.

A relationship also exists between the size of the production unit (the plant) and the cost of production. If the average cost of production per unit decreases as the size of the plant increases, economies of scale result, i.e., increasing returns to scale. Economists refer to constant, increasing, or decreasing returns to scale if, when all inputs are increased in a given proportion, the output of the commodity increases in the same, in a greater, or in a smaller proportion, respectively.

110

Exhibit E-1
Productivity Curves

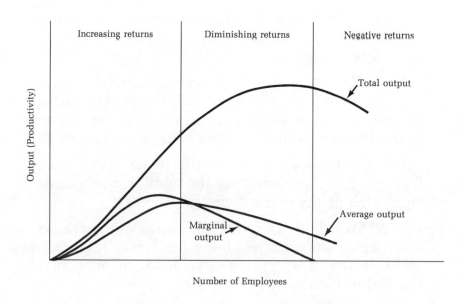

See also Break-even analysis; Goals and objectives; Performance evaluation; Benefit-cost analysis.

REFERENCE
Rayburn, L. Gayle, *Principles of Cost Accounting With Managerial Applications* (Irwin, Homewood, IL, 1979).

ELEMENTS OF FINANCIAL STATEMENTS
Elements of financial statements are described as the building blocks with which financial statements are constructed, that is, the classes of items that financial statements comprise. There are currently ten interrelated elements that are directly related

to measuring performance and status of an enterprise as defined in the FASB's Statement of Financial Accounting Concepts No. 3, Elements of Financial Statements of Business Enterprises:

ASSETS are probable future economic benefits obtained or controlled by a particular entity as a result of past transactions or events.

LIABILITIES are probable future sacrifices of economic benefits arising from present obligations of a particular entity to transfer assets or provide services to other entities in the future as a result of past transactions or events.

EQUITY is the residual interest in the assets of an entity that remains after deducting its liabilities. In a business entity, the equity is the ownership interest.

INVESTMENTS BY OWNERS are increases in net assets of a particular enterprise resulting from transfers to it from other entities of something of value to obtain or increase ownership interests (or equity) in it.

DISTRIBUTIONS TO OWNERS are decreases in net assets of a particular enterprise resulting from transferring assets, rendering services, or incurring liabilities by the enterprise to owners. Distributions to owners decrease ownership interest (or equity) in an enterprise.

COMPREHENSIVE INCOME is the change in equity (net assets) of an entity during a period from transactions and other events and circumstances from nonowner sources. It includes all changes in equity during a period except those resulting from investments by owners and distributions to owners.

REVENUES are inflows or other enhancements of assets of an entity or settlement of its liabilities (or a combination of both) during a period from delivering or producing goods, rendering services, or other activities that constitute the entity's ongoing major or central operations.

EXPENSES are outflows or other using up of assets or incurrence of liabilities during a period from delivering or producing goods or rendering services, or carrying out other activities that constitute the entity's ongoing major or central operations.

GAINS are increases in equity (net assets) from peripheral or incidental transactions of an entity and from all other transactions and other events and circumstances affecting the entity during a period except those that result from revenues or investments by owners.

LOSSES are decreases in equity (net assets) from peripheral or incidental transactions of an entity and from all other transactions and other events and circumstances affecting the entity during a period except those that result from expenses or distributions to owners.

See also Accounting; Revenue; Expense; Financial statements.

REFERENCE
SFAC No. 3, *Elements of Financial Statements of Business Enterprises* (FASB, Stamford, Conn., 1978).

ETHICS
Most if not all management functions (i.e., planning, controlling, directing, evaluating, etc.) have an impact on human acts which make them subject to ethical rules or principles of behavior. Managers, administrators, executives, and others should act ethically in their various capacities.

Ethics has been defined as "that branch of philosophy which is the systematic study of reflective choice, of the standards of right and wrong by which it is to be guided, and of the goods toward which it may ultimately be directed" (Philip Wheelwright, *A Critical Introduction to Ethics*). This definition emphasizes deliberate choice, moral principles, and the consequences of decisions. In a broad sense, ethical behavior is (1) that which produces a good instead of an evil, or (2) that which conforms to moral principles.

Various theories have been proposed to explain ethical behavior. An imperatative theory (I. Kant) directs humans to act according to an ethical rule or principle and not to specific situations or consequences. The utilitarianism theory emphasizes the consequences of human acts and proposes that one should choose good consequences over evil consequences. Utilitarianism is sometimes expressed in terms of choosing that which provides the greatest happiness or pleasure. Other theories suggest that if all persons who had acted the same under similar circumstances had produced desirable consequences, then one should act in that manner under similar circumstances without requiring a reason for doing so. These theories are usually referred to as generalists.

The most basic requirement of any ethical system is rationality. Rationality implies that what is specified is in conformity with reason, is nondeceiving (honest and authentic), and is attainable. An ethical system must be based on reality and should reflect the highest goals or objectives knowable at the time and under the existing circumstances, i.e., virtue over vice. The value structure expressed in the system's standards should indicate the means of achieving the results it promises and allowances should be made for diversity (the exception rule).

The philosophical choice to be ethical requires that one be free and that one accept the responsibilities which freedom bestows. One should choose to be ethical if one experiences a need to justify one's life. Justification implies living in harmony with an ideal deemed to have a positive value (i.e., honesty over dishonesty). Adhering to a value system provides continuity (consistent behavior) and internal controls (self-discipline and personal responsibility).

Major factors influencing ethical behavior include the law, government regulation, social pressure, industry and company ethical code, and personal standards of members of an organization. Conceptual wisdom concerning ethical behavior in business organizations suggests that:

1. Top management should lead the way if ethical behavior is to be fostered within an organization.
2. Top executives generally recognize the social responsibilities of their organizations.
3. Management frequently equates ethical behavior with obeying the law and complying with government regulations.
4. The emphasis that businesses place on economic motives and results is a major cause of unethical behavior.
5. Managers prefer specific company and industry codes to general statements of ethical conduct.

See also Fraud; Government regulation.

REFERENCES
Buchholz, Rogene A., *Business Environment and Public Policy* (Prentice-Hall, Englewood Cliffs, NJ, 1982).
Stoner, James A.F., *Management* (Prentice-Hall, Englewood Cliffs, NJ, 1982).

EXPENSE

Expenses are outflows or other using up of assets or incurrence of liabilities (or a combination of both) during a period from delivering or producing goods, rendering services, or carrying out other activities that constitute the entity's ongoing major or central operations.

Expenses represent actual or expected cash outflows that have occurred or will eventually occur as a result of the enterprise's ongoing major or central operations during a period. The matching principle of accounting requires that expenses be matched with revenues whenever it is reasonable and practicable. Three major expense recognition principles have been established for determining the accounting period in which expenses are recognized and reported:

1. Associating cause and effect. Some costs are recognized as expenses on the basis of a presumed direct association with specific revenues. For example, a sale of a product involves both sales revenue and cost of goods sold. The cost of the goods sold would be recognized in the accounting period that the sales revenue was recognized.

2. Systematic and rational allocation. Where there is no cause and effect relationship, an attempt is made to associate costs in a systematic and rational manner with the products of the periods affected. Costs that are associated with periods in a systematic way include depreciation and amortization expenses.

3. Immediate recognition. Costs that cannot be related to revenues either by associating cause and effect or by systematic and rational allocation are recognized as expenses of the current period. Such costs could include auditor's fee, research and development costs, and officers' salaries.

Expenses are classified on a multistep income statement in various categories. Operating expenses are usually reported in two categories: (1) selling expenses and (2) general and administrative expenses. Selling expenses include expenses associated with the sales function, such as sales salaries, advertising, store supplies used, and delivery expenses. General and administrative expenses are those expenses generally associated with the general operations of the enterprise. General and administrative expenses include officers' and office salaries, office supplies used, depreciation of office furniture, telephone, postage, legal and accounting services, and contributions. Other expenses include those identified with financial management and miscellaneous activities. Such expenses include interest expense and the write-down of obsolete inventory.

Expenses never include such items as dividend payments, repayment of loan principal, and expenditures to acquire items having future value (assets) to an enterprise.

The term *cost* should not be used to refer to expense. An expense is an expired cost. A cost can refer to an item that has service potential (an asset). An expense would arise when the cost no longer has service potential.

See also Income statement; Elements of financial statements; Revenue; Income.

REFERENCE
SFAC No. 3, *Elements of Financial Statements of Business Enterprises* (FASB, 1981).

F

FINANCIAL ACCOUNTING

Financial accounting is a subset of financial reporting that is primarily concerned with measuring and reporting financial information in a set of basic general-purpose financial statements. Financial accounting is designed primarily to meet the needs of external users of the financial statements of an enterprise. General purpose financial statements are statements designed to reasonably meet the needs of most users, primarily investors and creditors. Managerial accounting is concerned primarily with internal reporting. It relates essentially to planning, controlling, evaluating performance, and product costing for income valuation and income determination. There is some overlap between financial accounting and managerial accounting.

See also Accounting; Financial statements; Financial reporting; Objectives of financial reporting.

FINANCIAL FORECAST

A financial forecast for an enterprise is an estimate of the most probable financial position, results of operations and changes in financial position for one or more future periods. Most probable means that the forecast is based on management's judgment of the most likely set of conditions and its most likely course of action. A financial projection is an estimate of financial results based on assumptions which are not necessarily the most likely (SOP 75-4). A financial projection is sometimes used to present hypothetical courses of action for evaluation. A feasibility study is an analysis of a proposed investment or course of action (SOP 75-4).

A financial forecast presents a prediction of an entity's expected financial position, results of operations, and changes in financial position. A forecast is based on assumptions about expected conditions and expected courses of action, prepared to the best of the preparer's knowledge and belief. A financial projection differs from a financial forecast in that a projection depends upon one or more hypothetical assumption(s). A hypothetical assumption expresses a condition or course of action which is consistent with the purpose of the projection, but which does not necessarily reflect what the preparer expects to occur. A projection responds to the question: "What might happen if. . .?" Multiple projections consist of two or more projections based on a range of hypothetical assumptions.

Public accountants are primarily associated with forecasts and projects to lend their credibility to them. A client typically initiates the request that the accountant compile or review prospective financial information. In a review engagement, the accountant performs some procedures to achieve a level of assurance on which he/she bases an opinion. The accountant must perform inquiry and analytical procedures to achieve a reasonable basis for expressing limited assurance that there are no material modifications that should be made to the statements in order for them to be in conformity with generally accepted accounting principles or, if applicable, with another comprehensive basis of accounting. In a compilation service, the accountant performs few, if any, procedures; the accountant merely assists the client to "writeup" the financial information. Accountants are expected to render a report on compiled or reviewed prospective financial statements. The compilation report contains a disclaimer and offers no conclusions or any form of assurance. The review report gives the accountant's conclusions about proper presentation and about the reasonableness of the assumptions. The reports are either unqualified, adverse, or disclaimers resulting from scope limitations.

AICPA Rule of Conduct 201(e) prohibits an accountant from being associated with a forecast or projection which may lead readers to believe that the accountant vouches for the authenticity of the forecast or projection.

See also Budget; Decision making; Planning function; Control function; Financial planning.

REFERENCES

Burton, John C., et al., eds. *Handbook of Accounting and Auditing* (Warren, Gorham & Lamont, Boston, 1981).

Auditing Standards Board, *Statement on Standards for Accountants' Services on Prospective Financial Information—Financial Forecasts and Projections* (AICPA, New York, 1986).

FINANCIAL PLANNING

Personal financial planning involves the evaluation of a person's current financial position and financial goals leading to a presentation of a plan to achieve those goals. A typical financial plan includes the following:

1. A balance sheet analysis

2. Projection of cash flow

3. Long-term accumulation plans for retirement, education, etc.

4. Statement of individual's goals

5. Insurance analysis

6. Estate and tax planning

7. Projection of income taxes

8. Overview of weaknesses and strengths in the individual's financial outlook

9. Recommendations for implementing the plan

Financial planners charge clients in one of three major ways: a fee-only basis, a fee-and-commission basis, or on a commission basis.

Currently two professional organizations accredit planners after they have completed certain educational and professional requirements: the College for Financial Planning confers the Certified Financial Planner (CFP), and the American College confers the Chartered Financial Consultant (ChFC) designation. Two major professional organizations are associated with financial planning: the International Association for Financial Planning and the Institute of Certified Financial Planners.

See also Budget; Cash budget; Cash management; Forecast.

REFERENCE
Bailard, Thomas E., et al., *Personal Money Management* (Science Research Associates, Chicago, 1986).

FINANCIAL REPORTING

Financial reporting includes not only financial statements but also other means of communicating information that relates, directly or indirectly, to the information provided by the accounting system. Financial reporting is intended primarily to provide information that is useful in making business and economic decisions.

Financial reporting is a broad concept encompassing financial statements, notes to financial statements (and parenthetical disclosures), supplementary information (such as changing prices disclosures and oil and gas reserves information), and other means of financial reporting (such as management discussion and analysis, and letters to stockholders).

F

Financial reporting is but one source of information needed by those who make economic decisions about business enterprises. Exhibit F-1 shows the relationship of financial reporting to other information useful for investment, credit, and similar decisions.

The primary focus of financial reporting is information about earnings and its components. Information about earnings based on accrual accounting usually provides a better indication of an enterprise's present and continuing ability to generate positive cash flows than that provided by cash receipts and payments.

See also Accounting; Objectives of financial reporting; Financial accounting; Financial statements; Accounting basis.

REFERENCE
No. 1, *Objectives of Financial Reporting by Business Enterprises* (FASB, 1978).

FINANCIAL STATEMENT ANALYSIS

The purpose of financial statement analysis is to examine past and current financial data so that a company's performance and financial position can be evaluated and future risks and potential estimated. Financial statement analysis can yield valuable information about trends and relationships, the quality of a company's earnings, and the strengths and weaknesses of its financial position.

Creditors, investors, potential investors, and others are interested in evaluating a company's financial statements. Creditors are usually interested in knowing whether a company has the ability to meet its obligations as they mature and whether the long-term solvency of the company is assured. They are also interested in knowing the sources of a debtor's capital, how it has been invested, and how it is being employed. Investors and potential investors are primarily interested in evaluating the investment characteristics of a

Exhibit F-1
Relationship of Financial Reporting to Other Information Sources

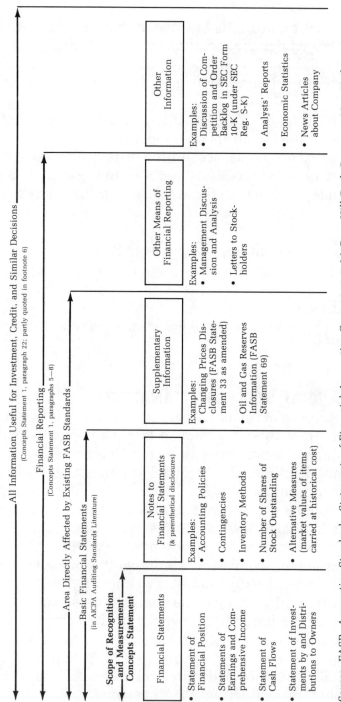

All Information Useful for Investment, Credit, and Similar Decisions
(Concepts Statement 1, paragraph 22; partly quoted in footnote 6)

Financial Reporting
(Concepts Statement 1, paragraphs 5—8)

Area Directly Affected by Existing FASB Standards

Basic Financial Statements
(in AICPA Auditing Standards Literature)

Scope of Recognition and Measurement Concepts Statement

Financial Statements

- Statement of Financial Position
- Statements of Earnings and Comprehensive Income
- Statement of Cash Flows
- Statement of Investments by and Distributions to Owners

Notes to Financial Statements
(& parenthetical disclosures)

Examples:
- Accounting Policies
- Contingencies
- Inventory Methods
- Number of Shares of Stock Outstanding
- Alternative Measures (market values of items carried at historical cost)

Supplementary Information

Examples:
- Changing Prices Disclosures (FASB Statement 33 as amended)
- Oil and Gas Reserves Information (FASB Statement 69)

Other Means of Financial Reporting

Examples:
- Management Discussion and Analysis
- Letters to Stockholders

Other Information

Examples:
- Discussion of Competition and Order Backlog in SEC Form 10-K (under SEC Reg. S-K)
- Analysts' Reports
- Economic Statistics
- News Articles about Company

Source: FASB, *Accounting Standards: Statements of Financial Accounting Concepts 1-6*, McGraw-Hill Book Company, New York, 1986.

company, including the relationship of the current value of a company's stock to expectations of its future value, the safety of their investment, the dividend policy of the company, the company's growth potential, and how the managers have carried out their stewardship function.

Financial statement analysis begins with establishing the objective(s) of the analysis. For example, is the analysis undertaken to provide a basis for granting credit or making an investment? After the objective of the analysis is established, the data is accumulated from the financial statements and from other sources. The results of the analysis are summarized and interpreted. Conclusions are reached and a report is made to the person(s) for whom the analysis was undertaken.

To evaluate financial statements, a person must:

1. be acquainted with business practices;

2. understand the purpose, nature, and limitations of accounting;

3. be familiar with the terminology of business and accounting; and

4. be acquainted with the tools of financial statement analysis.

Financial analysis of a company should include an examination of the financial statements of the company, including notes to the financial statements, and the auditor's report. The auditor's report will state whether the financial statements have been audited in accordance with generally accepted auditing standards. The report also indicates whether the statements fairly present the company's financial position, results of operations, and changes in financial position in accordance with generally accepted accounting principles. Notes to the financial statement are often more meaningful than the data found within the body of the statements. The notes explain the accounting policies of the company and usually provide detailed explanations of how those policies were applied along with supporting details. Analysts often compare the financial statements of one company with those of other companies in the same industry and with those of the industry in which the company operates as well as with prior year statements of the company being analyzed.

Comparative financial statements provide analysts with significant information about trends and relationships over two or more years. Comparative statements are considerably more significant for evaluating a company than are single-year statements. Financial statement ratios are additional tools for analyzing financial statements. Financial ratios establish relationships between various items appearing on financial statements. Ratios can be classified as follows:

1. *Liquidity ratios.* Measure the ability of the enterprise to pay its debts as they mature.

2. *Activity (or turnover) ratios.* Measure how effectively the enterprise is using its assets.

3. *Profitability ratios.* Measure management's success in generating returns for those who provide capital to the enterprise.

4. *Coverage ratios.* Measure the protection for long-term creditors and investors.

The entry Ratios in this book provides a detailed overview of financial ratios.

Horizontal analysis and vertical analysis of financial statements are additional techniques that can be used effectively when evaluating a company. Horizontal analysis and vertical analysis are forms of percentage analysis.

Horizontal analysis spotlights trends and establishes relationships between items that appear on the same row of a comparative statement. Horizontal analysis discloses changes on items in financial statements over time. Each item (such as sales) on a row for one fiscal period is compared with the same item in a different period. Horizontal analysis can be carried out in terms of changes in dollar amounts, percentages of change, or in a ratio format.

Vertical analysis involves the conversion of items appearing in statement columns into terms of percentages of a base figure to show the relative significance of the items and to facilitate comparisons. For example, individual items appearing on the income statement can be expressed as percentages of sales. On the balance sheet, individual assets can be expressed as a percentage of total assets. Liabilities and owners' equity accounts can be expressed in terms of their relationship to total liabilities and owners' equity. Statements omitting dollar amounts and showing only percentages can be prepared. Such statements are referred to as "common size statements" because each item in the statement has a common basis for comparison, for example, total assets, net sales.

Investors and creditors should be interested not only in the quantity of an enterprise's assets and earnings but in their quality as well. The quality of assets refers to whether a company has a well-balanced composition of assets, their condition, liquidity, and profitability. How well are the plant and equipment maintained? How salable is the inventory? What is the relationship between debt and stockholders' equity? The quality of earnings is related to the amount and stability of earnings, the security of the source(s) of earnings, the rate of earnings on sales, total assets, owners' equity, and the accounting methods used to measure income (conservative or otherwise).

Financial statement analysis has its limitations. Statements represent the past and do not necessarily predict the future. However, financial statement analysis can provide clues or suggest a need for further investigation. What is found on financial statements is the product of accounting conventions and procedures (LIFO or FIFO inventory; straight-line or accelerated depreciation) that sometimes distort the economic reality

129

or substance of the underlying situation. Financial statements say little directly about changes in markets, the business cycle, technological developments, laws and regulations, management personnel, price-level changes, and other critical analytical concerns.

See also Ratios; Financial statements; Break-even analysis; Gross margin analysis; Contribution-margin analysis; Liquidity; Leverage.

REFERENCE
Bernstein, Leopold A., *Financial Statement Analysis: Theory, Application, and Interpretation* (Richard D. Irwin, Homewood, IL, 1983).

FINANCIAL STATEMENTS
Financial statements are the most widely used and the most comprehensive way of communicating financial information to users of the information provided on the reports. Different users of financial statements have different informational needs. General-purpose financial statements have been developed to meet the needs of the users of financial statements, primarily the needs of investors and creditors.

The basic output of the financial accounting process is presented in the following interrelated general purpose financial statements:

1. A balance sheet (or statement of financial position) summarizes the financial position of an accounting entity at a particular point in time.

2. An income statement summarizes the results of operations for a given period of time.

3. A statement of changes in financial position summarizes an enterprise's financing and investing activities over a given period of time.

4. A statement of retained earnings shows the increases and decreases in earnings retained by the company over a given period of time. This statement is sometimes combined with the income statement. The statement of retained earnings is sometimes expanded into a statement of stockholders' equity that discloses changes in other stockholders' equity accounts in addition to retained earnings.

Notes to financial statements are considered an integral part of a complete set of financial statements.

The major financial statements are interrelated (or articulate) with each other. The income statement and the statement of changes in financial position can be viewed as connecting links between the beginning and ending statements of financial position. The income statement basically describes the changes in the statement of financial position accounts that result from operations. The statement of changes in financial position explains changes in the balance sheet of cash or working capital between two points in time. Exhibit F-2 shows graphically the interrelationship of the financial statements.

Financial statements can be presented in various ways including the following: general purpose financial statements; classified; comparative; annual or interim; consolidated; combined; constant dollar; common size:

1. General-purpose financial statements are reports published by a company for use by persons who do not have the ability to obtain specialized financial reports designed to meet their interests. Such statements include the balance sheet, income statement, statement of retained earnings, and the statement of changes in financial position.

2. Classified financial statements separate the major items appearing on financial statements into subcategories. For example, a classified balance sheet divides assets,

Exhibit F-2
Interrelationship, or Articulation, of Financial Statements

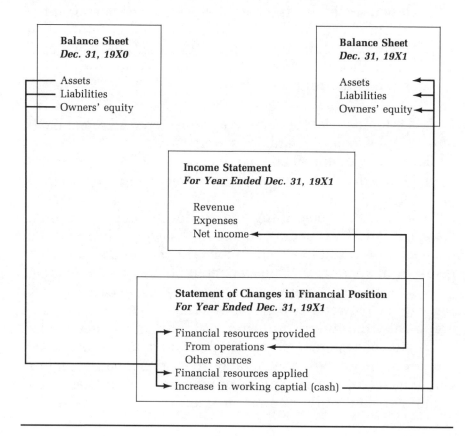

liabilities, and owners' equity into subclassifications.

3. Comparative statements present data for two or more successive accounting periods placed in columns side by side to disclose trends and relationships.

4. Annual statements give information for a fiscal year; interim statements disclose information for a period less than a year, such as quarterly or monthly statements.

5. Consolidated statements present information about legally separate companies as though they were a single entity, for example, a parent company and its subsidiaries. Combined statements are similar to consolidated statements except that intercompany transactions are not eliminated.

6. Constant dollar statements are financial statements in which the monetary units are restated so as to represent the same general purchasing power.

7. Common size statements are prepared using percentages instead of dollars; for example, individual items on a balance sheet could be shown as a percentage of total assets, and items on an income statement could be shown as a percentage of net sales.

See also Objectives of financial reporting; Qualitative characteristics of accounting information; Financial accounting; Financial reporting; Working capital; Revenue; Expense; Financial statement analysis.

REFERENCE
SFAC No. 1, *Objectives of Financial Reporting by Business Enterprises* (FASB, 1978).

FIXED AND FLEXIBLE BUDGETS
A fixed, or static, budget is a planning document that assumes or estimates a volume prior to the beginning of the budget period. The budget is dependent upon the selection of the estimated volume and is not adjusted when actual volume differs from the estimated volume.

A flexible, or variable, budget is defined as one that can be adjusted to show what revenue and expenses should have been at the actual volume achieved. Flexible budgets are ordinarily more valid for comparing budgets with actual results than are fixed budgets. Flexible budgets are used primarily for control purposes, including variance analysis and performance evaluation. A flexible budget is illustrated here. The basic budget formula for overhead is $3.75 per unit and $800 per month. Three possible volumes within the relevant range of this cost center are shown. Budgets at other volume levels would be computed in a similar manner.

Cost Center ABC
Variable Budget
Factory Overhead
January 2, 19--

	1,500	2,000	2,500	
Production units	1,500	2,000	2,500	
Variable costs				
Indirect materials	$1,500	$2,000	$2,500	$1.00 per unit
Indirect labor	2,000	4,000	5,000	2.00 per unit
Supplies	750	1,000	1,250	.50 per unit
Total variable costs	$4,250	$7,000	$8,250	3.75 per unit
Fixed costs:				
Depreciation	$ 500	$ 500	$ 500	$500 per month
Insurance	300	300	300	300 per month
Total fixed costs	$ 800	$ 800	$ 800	$800 per month
Total overhead	$5,050	$7,800	$9,050	

See also Budgets; Cost behavior.

FLOWCHARTS

A flowchart is a symbolic, diagrammatic representation of a sequential flow. Flowcharting enables the preparer and user to understand a system, to communicate a description of the system to others, and to evaluate the system.

Defined symbols are used to show steps and actions. Flow lines are used to indicate how documents and records are related. Arrowheads indicate the direction of the flow, except down and to the right. Areas of responsibility are established as vertical columns or sections through which the flow of documents occurs horizontally (from left to right). Exhibit F-3 shows the basic symbols widely used in flowcharting. Exhibit F-4 shows a flowchart of sales, billing, and shipping departments of a small wholesale company.

See also Planning function; Control function.

FORECAST

A forecast is a technique which purports to estimate some aspect of the future. Forecasting business activity consists of:

1. understanding the reason(s) for past changes,
2. determining which phase or activity of business should be measured,
3. selecting and compiling data which is to be used for measuring, and
4. analyzing and interpreting the data.

Forecasting future activity is related to measuring changes in business activity. Forecasters frequently classify data on the basis of intervals of time, since this is usually an effective method of identifying changes that have occurred. Data classified according to periods of time can be classified according to type of economic change:

1. Secular trend.
2. Seasonal variation.
3. Cyclical fluctuations.
4. Random or erratic fluctuation.

Secular trends refer to the effect of forces influencing growth or decline over relatively long periods of time. Seasonal variations represent regularly recurring or periodic movements with the seasons of the year. Cyclical movements refer to recurring changes that do not necessarily occur in a fixed period

Exhibit F-3
Flowcharting Symbols

Document – paper documents and
reports of all types
Example: a sales invoice

Process Symbol – any processing function;
defined operation causing a change in
value, form, or location of information
Example: a billing clerk prepares a sales invoice

Off-line Storage – off-line storage of
documents, records, and EDP files
Example: a duplicate sales invoice is filed
in numerical order

Transmittal Tape – a proof or adding machine
tape used for control purposes
Example: an adding machine tape of sales invoices

Input/Output Symbol – used to indicate
information entering or leaving system
Example: a receipt of order from customer

Decision – used to indicate a decision is made
requiring different action for a yes or no answer
(this symbol is rarely used)
Example: is customer credit satisfactory

No

Yes

Annotation – the addition of descriptive
comments or explanatory notes as clarification
Example: a billing clerk checks credit before
preparing an invoice

Directional Flow–Lines – the direction of
processing or data flow

Connector – exit to, or entry from, another part
of chart; keyed in by using numbers
Example: a document transfer from one department
into another department

Symbols Unique to EDP Systems

Punched Card	Punched Tape	Magnetic Tape	Disk or Drum Storage

Source: Alvin A. Arens and James K. Loebbecke, *Auditing: An Integrated Approach*, Prentice-Hall, Englewood Cliffs, NH, 1980.

Exhibit F–4
Flowcharting of Sales

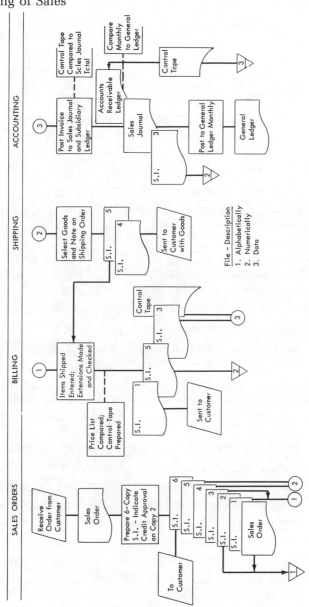

Source: Alvin A. Arens and James K. Loebbecke, *Auditing: An Integrated Approach*, Prentice-Hall, Englewood Cliffs, NJ, 1986.

of time, e.g., as in a business cycle with periods of depression, recovery, prosperity, and recession. Random movements refer to small variations that are typically random or erratic in nature, resulting from many factors which are usually not considered important.

There are three basic methods of forecasting:

1. *Qualitative methods.* Qualitative methods of forecasting rely primarily on human judgment, including logical, unbiased, and systematic techniques. The Delphi method of forecasting is an example. Under this method, a forecasting group performs a succession of repeated brainstorming rounds which produce, develop, and comment on the ideas of others until a consensus is reached. The name refers to the oracle of Apollo, near Delphi in Greece.

2. *Casual methods.* Casual methods forecast about one or more known factor (an independent variable) to predict the value of another factor (a dependent variable). For example, the demand for a product might be casually related to the gross national product. Forecasting sales in budgeting often is based on historical projections which assumes there is a causal relationship between past sales trends and future sales. Correlation models are sometimes used to develop the relationship.

3. *Time series methods.* A time series is a set of data arranged chronologically. Underlying time patterns include trends, seasonal variations, cycle, and randomness. Indexes and regression models are sometimes used to develop the relationship.

Significant methods of analysis used to summarize the characteristics of one time series include:

1. *Secular trend:* linear or nonlinear least squares method or moving average method. For example, linear, least

squares method, odd number of time periods:

$$Y' = a + bX \qquad a = \frac{\Sigma Y}{N} \qquad b = \frac{\Sigma XY}{\Sigma X^2}$$

where

Y' = trend value
a = average (arithemetic mean) trend value
b = rate of change in trend
X = any time value
ΣY = sum of values of variable
N = Number of time periods for which there are observations
ΣXY = Sum of products formed by multiplying the value of each Y by each corresponding X
ΣX^2 = Sum of all X's after they have been squared

2. *Seasonal variations:* indexes, e.g., ratio to moving average method.
Formula:
$$S = \frac{T \times C \times S}{T \times C}$$

where

S = seasonal value
T = secular trend value
C = cycle value
$T \times C \times S$ = Original data
$T \times C$ = trend and cycle measurement

3. *Cyclical movement:*
Formula:
$$C \times R = \frac{T \times C \times S \times R}{T \times S}$$

where

T = Secular trend value
C = Cycle value
S = Seasonal index
R = Value of random element

Significant methods of analysis used to study the variations in one series as related to variations in another series include:

1. *Regression analysis:* a procedure which uses a known variable and an unknown variable to estimate the unknown variable, i.e., how the variables are related, e.g., linear and nonlinear regression.

$$X_1 = b_{11} + b_{12}X_2 + b_{13}X_3$$

where

X_1 = any value of dependent variable on the net regression line (same as Y' used on page 45)

b_{11} = point of intersection of the regression lines of the planes

b_{12} = rate of change in X_1 as X_2 changes

X_2 = any value of first independent variable

b_{13} = rate of change in X_1 as X_3 changes

X_3 = any value of second independent variable

Formula: linear relationships, more than one independent variable

2. *Correlation analysis:* a procedure for measuring the degree of relationship between two or more variables. The closer the relationship, the greater the confidence that can be placed in the estimate. Correlation analysis can be linear, nonlinear, multiple, partial, or rank correlation.

Formula:

$$r = \frac{N\Sigma XY - (\Sigma X)(\Sigma Y)}{[N\Sigma X^2 - (\Sigma X)^2][N\Sigma Y^2 - (\Sigma Y)^2]}$$

where

r = coefficient of correlation

$N\Sigma XY$ = Multiply each X by each corresponding Y. Add these products. Then multiply this sum by N, the total number of paired observations.

$(\Sigma X)(\Sigma Y)$ = Add all X values. Add all Y values. Multiply sum of X values by sum of Y values.

$N\Sigma X^2$ = square each X value. Add squared X values. Multiply this sum by N, the total number of paired observations.
$(\Sigma X)^2$ = Add all X values. Square this sum.
$N\Sigma Y^2$ = Square each Y value. Add squares. Multiply sum by N.
$(\Sigma Y)^2$ = Add all Y values. Square sum.

The quality of a forecast is evaluated in terms of bias and precision. *Bias* indicates whether forecasts are consistently higher or lower than observations. *Precision* is a measure of variability in the forecast error.

Forecasts can be monitored by using a data filter test and a tracking signal test. The data signal test is used to detect unusual occurrences, such as clerical errors or unexpected large changes in the data pattern. The tracking signal test is used to identify a basic change in the data pattern and other changes.

See also Budget; Comprehensive budget; Financial forecast; Forecasting financial requirements.

REFERENCES
Fallon, William K., ed., *AMA Management Handbook* (AMACOM, New York, 1983).
Makridakis, S., and Wheelwright, S. C., *Forecasting, TIMS Studies in Management Studies*, vol. 12, 1980.

FORECASTING FINANCIAL REQUIREMENTS
Working capital is the basis for forecasting financial requirements. A percentage of sales approach, using financial ratios, can be used to forecast financial requirements.

To illustrate forecasting financial requirements, assume that the data in Exhibit F-5 is available. The company wants to know what amount of additional financing is required if sales are expected to reach the $600,000 level (a 20 percent increase). The percentage of sales approach will be used to provide the answer.

Exhibit F-5
Hypothetical Data for Financial Forecasting Case

Assets		Liabilities and owners' equity	
Cash	$ 10,000	Accounts payable	$ 50,000
Receivables	30,000	Notes payable	150,000
Inventory	60,000	Common stock	100,000
Plant and		Retained earnings	200,000
equipment (net)	400,000		
Total assets	$500,000		$500,000

Additional data:

Sales	$500,000
Net income	50,000
Profit margin on sales	10%
Plant capacity utilized	100%
Dividend payout rate	25% of net income
	(earnings retention rate is 75%)

Step 1. What balance sheet items vary directly with sales? Assume that the assets and accounts payable vary directly with sales.

Step 2. Express the balance sheet items that vary directly with sales as a percentage of sales ($500,000).

Cash	2.0	Accounts payable	10.0
Receivables	6.0		
Inventory	12.0		
Plant and equipment	80.0		
Total	100.0		10.0
Assets as a percent of sales			100.0
Less: available credit from suppliers			10.0
Percentage of each additional sales dollar to be financed			90.0

For each $1.00 of sales, assets will increase $1.00. This increase must be financed. Accounts payable are assumed to be financed by suppliers who make credit available and so provide 10 percent of new funds. The firm must find additional financing from internal or external sources for 90 percent of each sales dollar.

If sales are to increase from $500,000 to $600,000, then $90,000 (= $100,000 increase in sales × 90%) in new funds are required.

Step 3. How much of the financing required ($90,000) can be financed internally from operations?

Since the sales revenue will be $600,000 and the profit margin is 10 percent, profit will be $60,000. Of this amount, $15,000 is required for dividends ($60,000 × 25% dividend payout). This leaves $45,000 of net income available to finance some of the additional sales.

Step 4. How much of the financing requirement must be financed externally?

If $45,000 of the $90,000 total requirement is provided internally, then $45,000 must be obtained from external sources. The relationships reflected in this illustration can be summarized in the following formula:

External funds needed = (A/TR)(S)-(B/TR)(S)-bm(Q)

where

A/TR = assets that increase spontaneously with total revenues or sales as a percentage of total revenues or sales,

B/TR = those liabilities that increase spontaneously with total revenues or sales as a percent of total revenue or sales

S = change in total revenue or sales
m = profit margin on sales
b = earnings retention ratio
Q = total revenues projected for the year

External funds required = $\underline{(\$500,000)}$ $(-\$100,000)$
($500,000)

$-\ \underline{(\$50,000)}$ $(-\$100,000)$
($500,000)

$-$ (75%) (10%) ($600,000)

$=$ $45,000 (same as computed in the discussion)

To summarize, the relationship between sales and assets is the key question in forecasting financing requirements. The formula used in this illustration can be used in different ways by changing the assumptions.

See also Forecast; Cash management; Financial forecast; Budget; Working capital; Ratios.

FRAUD

Fraud is a legal concept that requires a conscious knowledge of the falsity with deliberate intent to deceive. Fraud includes intentional deception, misappropriation of an enterprise's assets, and the manipulation of financial data to benefit the perpetrator (management or employee). Constructive fraud is a deceit that involves a false representation of a material fact without reasonable ground for belief that is relied on by another and results in his damage.

Psychoanalytic theory attributes fraud to an individual's (1) improper striving to satisfy basic needs and desires or (2) an underdeveloped, misformed, or erroneous conscience. Sociologists explain fraud in terms of environmental factors, including social influences and personal interactions (i.e., criminal or deviant behavior is learned). Some moralists explain fraud in terms of failures or inadequacies in moral development and behavior.

Fraud deterrence and deterrence programs must take into consideration:

1. Environmental pressures (excessive debt; financial losses; unrealistic company goals and objectives, etc.),

2. Targets of opportunity, and

3. The personality and character of the defrauder.

Major deterrents to fraudulent activities are (1) fear of detection and punishment and (2) the moral effect of unethical actions on the perpetrator. The fear factor is associated with the threat and effect of detection and punishment.

A reliable fraud deterrence program should be built around these barriers to fraudulent acts:

1. a well-designed organizational structure

2. sound and comprehensive internal control policies and procedures

3. competent, responsible, and alert management and supervisions

4. aware and concerned corporate directors, audit committees, and corporate officers

5. competent, creative, and aggressive audit surveillance

6. comprehensive policies and procedures for dealing with fraud

7. high moral and ethical standards of officers, employees, and auditors

The discovery of fraud can be approached logically from a search for the perpetrator's:

1. motive: reason or incentive that moves a person to action;

2. method: plan, procedure, process; and

3. opportunity: circumstances favorable for the purpose.

The adequacy of performance by an auditor relates primarily to the professional skill, judgment, and knowledge generally required of professional auditors. Ranges of misrepresentation include negligence (belief without adequate basis), constructively fraudulent (without belief in a position taken), and fraudulent (known to be false). The auditor's reliance on a company's internal control procedures makes the discovery of certain types of fraud more difficult. Furthermore, the concept of materiality can also affect fraud detection because items that are not material to the financial statements are not always examined or are merely sampled.

The Commission on Auditors' Responsibilities addressed the question of an auditor's responsibility to a client for fraud of client personnel as follows:

"Under generally accepted auditing standards the independent auditor has the responsibility, within the inherent limitations of the auditing process. . . to plan his examination. . . to search for errors or irregularities that would have a material effect on the financial statements, and to exercise due skill and care in the conduct of the examination. The auditor's search for material errors or irregularities ordinarily is accomplished by the performance of those auditing procedures that in his judgment are appropriate in the circumstances to form an opinion on the financial statements; extended auditing procedures are required if the auditor's examination indicates that material errors or irregularities may exist. . . An independent auditor's standard report implicitly indicates his belief that the financial statements taken as a whole are not materially misstated as a result of errors or irregularities."

In tax law, tax fraud falls into two categories: civil and criminal. For civil fraud, the Internal Revenue Service can impose as a penalty an amount equal to 50 percent of the underpayment. For criminal tax fraud, fines and/or imprisonment is prescribed for conviction of various types of fraud. Conviction of civil and criminal fraud requires a specific intent on the part of the taxpayer to evade the tax. Negligence alone is not sufficient. Criminal fraud also requires willfulness (deliberately and with evil purpose). The IRS has the burden of proving fraud.

See also Control function; Internal control; Ethics.

REFERENCE
Burton, John C., et al., eds., *Handbook of Accounting and Auditing* (Warren, Gorman & Lamont, Boston, 1981).

FREE ENTERPRISE SYSTEM
In the United States, the free (or private) enterprise system is the basic economic system. In a free enterprise system,

1. private citizens are free to own and operate a business;

2. the means of production (land, factories, equipment) are privately owned, although government does own and operate some enterprises such as the postal system;

3. incentive for investors and business is the profit motive; and

4. competition is a characteristic of the marketplace.

The terms *capitalism* and *free enterprise* are often used interchangeably. Accounting serves the free enterprise economic system by providing financial data that can be used to make the economic choices that an enterprise or person must make, especially as these choices relate to the allocation of an enterprise's or investor's economic resources. Accounting also serves other economic systems.

REFERENCE
Baumol, W. J., and Blinder, Alan S., *Economics: Principles and Policy* (Harcourt Brace Jovanovich, San Diego, CA, 1986).

G

G

GOALS AND OBJECTIVES

The establishment of useful goals and objectives is the first step in the planning process. Goals are general statements of what the organization seeks to accomplish through its programs; objectives are specific statements which have the same purposes as goals. Successful organizations typically establish a formal process for establishing goals and objectives. (The relationship of goals and objectives to the planning and control process is shown in Exhibit C-19.)

The establishing of goals and objectives serves many purposes: identifies the basic ends and means to those ends; provides a sense of direction, decision guidelines, and performance criteria; and reduces uncertainty within the organization. Goals enable the enterprise to plan, act, evaluate, and revise so that the goals themselves will be realized. The stages of the planning process for reaching the goals and objectives are as follows:

1. Determine where the organization is now.

2. Know where it wants to be (ends; goals and objectives).

3. Select the appropriate ways for getting there with available resource (means).

G

A goal is a statement of where one wants to go or what one wants to achieve. It is the intended result of proposed activity. A goal statement can describe the intended result (make a profit) or indicate the direction that one's activity should take (increase profits; reduce costs). Because goals are general statements of an intended result (point the direction), it is usually necessary to express them more precisely in terms of one or more objectives. Objectives are more specific than goals; they usually specify a performance standard or criteria for results which can be observed or measured. The process of assessing goals and objectives will deal with such issues as:

1. What is to be accomplished?
2. Why is it to be undertaken?
3. What is expected of the parties involved?
4. How will one know when it is accomplished?

It is usually beneficial for an organization to have written goals and objectives:

1. to establish what the purpose of an undertaking is and to specify how it is to be accomplished,
2. to serve as a basis for establishing authority and responsibilities,
3. to establish priorities,
4. to determine performance standards, and
5. to communicate effectively the contribution and commitment required of all parties.

Because objectives deal with measurable performance results, obectives should specify:

1. the results to be obtained (one objective, one result),

2. the person who will evaluate the results,

3. the criteria that will be used to measure the results, and

4. the conditions for measuring results (when? where? how?).

Establishing goals and objectives implies that change in some form or other is required. To rationally consider what change is required, one needs to justify the intended result (end). Then one can determine the means (resources and processes) required to attain the end. A practical approach to resolving this issue is to determine (1) what is the current situation and (2) what should be.

An organization generally has many levels of goals and objectives. Top management has more goals and objectives than does middle management. However, goals and objectives established for the various levels must be integrated so that the entire effort of the organization contributes to the final or ultimate goals of the entity. This concept is usually referred to as *goal congruence*. Goal congruence means that the goals, objectives, and actions of all members of an organization are in agreement with or conform to the goals, objectives, and actions of the organization. Maximizing goal congruences begins with the establishment of long-range goals and objectives in the strategic planning process. Goal congruence encourages all levels of management to keep the "big picture" in focus at all times.

Organizations typically have multiple goals which may conflict, e.g., market share and profit maximization. Managers generally deal with goal conflicts in one of the following ways:

1. Agree to accept a satisfactory rather than a maximum level of performance, i.e., satisficing.

2. Establish a hierarchy among the goals which requires that a satisfactory level of achievement be attained on

G

the more important goals before dealing with less important ones.

3. Continually revaluate and, if necessary, revise goals.

Criteria for effective objectives include suitability, feasibility, acceptability, achievability, measurability, adaptability, cost effectiveness, and commitment by management to the attainment of the objectives.

See also Organizing function; Performance evaluation; Planning function; Control function; Motivation.

REFERENCE
Steiss, Alan Walter, *Strategic Management and Organizational Decision Making* (Lexington Books, Lexington, MA, 1985).

GOVERNMENT REGULATION

Relations between business and government in the United States are generally described as adversarial in nature, a condition which requires corporate managers to become political strategists. In Europe and Japan, a partnership or cooperative approach is often encountered. The adversarial approach to government regulation, which employs a command and control system, is often counter-productive and ineffective.

A strategic response to regulation requires an awareness, commitment, policy evaluation and selection, and implementation. Strategic responses include opportunism, stonewalling, cooperation, pragmatism, and others.

The regulatory trend in the United States has been toward social regulation while still retaining a strong degree of economic regulation (competitive behavior and industry regulation). Social regulators include the Environmental Protection Agency, the Occupational Safety and Health Administration, the Consumer Product Safety Commission, and others. Economic regulators include the Federal Trade Commission, Civil

Aeronautics Board, Federal Communications Commission, the Interstate Commerce Commission, and others. Public policy issues related to regulation cluster around antitrust policies, equality of economic opportunity, equality of employment opportunity, occupational safety and health, consumerism, and the physical environment.

The State Governmental Affairs Committee described a federal regulatory office as "one which (1) had decision making authority, (2) establishes standards or guidelines conferring benefits and imposing restrictions on business conduct, (3) operates principally in the sphere of domestic business activity, (4) has its head and/or members appointed by the president. . . and (5) has its legal procedures generally governed by the Administrative Procedures Act."

Congress has passed major antitrust laws which have for their purpose the maintenance of competition and the prevention of restraint of trade. This legislation also restricts unfair competitive practices.

The Sherman Antitrust Act declared that "every contract, combination. . . or conspiracy in restraint of trade or commerce among the several states is hereby declared to be illegal"; and "every person who shall monopolize, or. . . combine or conspire to monopolize any part of the trade or commerce among the several states. . . shall be deemed guilty of a misdemeanor. . ." Courts have generally held that the restraint must be "undue" and "unreasonable" before it is considered to be illegal. The courts have held that bigness in and of itself is not proof of violation. The "principle of reason" has to be applied to such cases. Specifically, the Sherman Act prohibited price discrimination when it tends to lessen competition in any line of commerce. The Act also forbids sellers from requiring buyers to refrain from buying the goods of their rivals when such a policy tends to create a monopoly, e.g., certain tying arrangements and exclusive dealing arrangements.

The Clayton Act, passed in 1914, was directed at the tendency toward corporate combinations which restrained trade or commerce. As it relates to antitrust matters, the Clayton Act states that "Unfair methods of competition in or affecting commerce, and unfair or deceptive acts or practices in or affecting commerce are hereby declared unlawful." Specifically, the act prohibits (1) price discriminations that would result in a lessening of competition or tend to create monopoly; (2) tying clauses in contracts which required buyers of products not to use the product of a competitor of the seller; (3) the acquisition of the stock of one corporation by a competing corporation for the purpose of lessening competition; and (4) interlocking directorates. Recent developments in 1977 in antitrust legislation raised the penalty for violations from misdemeanors to a felony punishable by fines not exceeding $1 million for a corporation or $100,000 for an individual and imprisonment not exceeding three years.

The Clayton Act was amended in 1936 when the Robinson-Patman Act was passed. The Robinson-Patman Act was designed to prevent "unfair" competition in trade by giving or receiving discounts or services when such acts amounted to discrimination and in a substantial reduction of competition. Price discrimination can occur when a supplier sells the same product to two different competitive wholesales at different prices, when the effect may be to injure competition. The Act also makes it illegal for a buyer to knowingly induce or receive a discriminatory, lower price. Price differentials can be legal if (1) they do not injure competition, (2) they result from cost differences in selling to different customers, (3) they are used to sell obsolete products, (4) they are offered in good faith to meet a competitor's price, and (5) they are offered to noncompeting customers. The Act also prohibits sellers from offering various types of advertising or promotional allowances unless they offer them to all customers "on proportionately equal terms."

The Robinson-Patman Act was amended in 1950 by the Anti-Merger Act, or the Celler-Kefauver Amendment, which makes it illegal for one corporation to acquire the assets of another company where the acquisition would substantially lessen competition, restrain commerce, or trend to create a monopoly.

The Federal Trade Commission Act of 1914 declares "that unfair methods of competition in commerce are hereby declared unlawful. The commission is hereby empowered and directed to precent persons, partnerships, corporations, except banks, and common carriers subject to the acts which regulate commerce, from using unfair methods in commerce." The Wheeler-Lea Act of 1938 empowered the Commission to restrain business practices that it considers harmful to the public interest, especially false advertising and the adulteration of manufactured products.

Alternatives to government regulation would include (1) greater freedom in allowing businesses to attain social objectives, (2) increased cooperation between business and government in establishing realistic performance standards, (3) a willingness on the part of business to acknowledge the legitimacy of social objectives, and (4) let the marketplace bring about desired changes in business behavior.

See also Pricing policy; Pricing policy: regulated prices; Ethics.

REFERENCE
Buchholz, Rogene A., Business Environment and Public Policy: Implications for Management (Prentice-Hall, Englewood Cliffs, NJ, 1982).

GROSS MARGIN ANALYSIS

Gross margin (or gross profit) is the excess of sales over cost of goods sold. Gross margin represents the dollar amount of financial resources produced by the basic selling activity of the firm. On an income statement, gross margin appears as follows:

	1991	1990	Change
Sales	$225,000	$100,000	$125,000
Cost of goods sold	90,000	50,000	40,000
GROSS MARGIN	135,000	50,000	85,000
Operating expenses	90,000	35,000	55,000
Net income	$ 45,000	$ 15,000	$ 30,000

G

Changes in gross margin from period to period may be due to any one or any combination of the following variables:

1. Change in sales caused by:

   a. change in selling price (sales-price variance);

   b. change in volume of goods sold (sales-volume variance).

2. Change in cost of goods sold caused by:

   a. change in unit cost (cost-price variance);

   b. change in volume of goods sold (cost-volume variance).

The four gross margin variances can be computed for year-to-year data using the following formulas and the following data which relate to the income statement shown earlier. The analysis which results from interpreting these variances is referred to as gross margin analysis.

	1991	1990
Number of units sold	150,000	100,000
Sales price per unit	$1.50	$1.00
Cost per unit	$0.60	$0.50

1. Sales-price variance = Current year's units sold × Change in sales price per unit
   - = 150,000 × $0.50
   - = $75,000 favorable variance

2. Sales-volume variance = Change in units sold × Last year's prices
   - = 50,000 units × $1.00
   - = $50,000 favorable variance

3. Cost-price variance = Current year's units sold × Change in cost per unit
   - = 150,000 × $0.10
   - = $15,000 unfavorable variance

4. Cost-volume variance = Change in units sold × Last year's cost
   - = 50,000 units × $0.50
   - = $25,000 unfavorable variance

When the four variances are combined, the $85,000 change in gross profit from 1990 to 1991 is identified:

Sales-price variance	$75,000
Sales-volume variance	50,000
Cost-price variance	(15,000)
Cost-volume variance	(25,000)
Change in gross margin	$85,000

For a multiproduct firm, a sales-mix variance is usually computed. This variance identifies the change in gross margin attributable to shifts in the sales mix for the company. This approximates the effect of changing the sales mix at a constant volume. This variance can be computed using the following formula:

$$\text{Sales-mix variance} = \text{Current year's sales} \times \text{Change in gross margin rate}$$
$$= \$225,000 \times (.60 - .50)$$
$$= \$22,500 \text{ favorable variance}$$

See also Contribution margin analysis.

I

I

IMPUTED AND IMPLICIT COSTS

Expenditures that are attributable to the use of one's own factor of production, such as the use of one's own capital, are imputed costs. In accounting, imputed costs are often ignored when recording transactions.

Interest imputation is the process that estimates the interest rate to be used in finding the cash price of an asset. An imputed interest rate is similar to an implicit interest rate in that it equates the present value of payments on a note with the face of the note, but it can also be established by factors not associated with the note transaction or underlying contract. The imputed rate approximates a negotiated rate (a fair market interest rate) between independent borrowers and lenders. The imputed rate takes into consideration the term of the note, the credit standing of the issuer, collateral, and other factors. For example, an investor is considering the purchase of a large tract of undeveloped land. The offering price is $450,000 in the form of a noninterest-bearing note that is to be paid in three yearly installments of $150,000. There is no market for the note or the property. When the investor considered the current prime rate, his credit standing, the collateral, other terms of the note, and rates available for similar borrowings, a 12 percent interest rate is imputed.

Implicit interest (versus imputed interest) is interest implied in a contract. Implicit interest is interest that is neither paid nor received. The implicit interest rate is the interest rate that equates the present value of payments on a note with the face of the note. The implicit rate is determined by factors directly related to the note transaction. For example, assume that a dealer offers to sell a machine for $100,000 cash or $16,275 per year for ten years. By dividing the cash price by the annual payments (an annuity), a factor of 6.144 is computed ($100,000/$16,275). By referring to a Present Value of an Annuity of 1 in Arrears table, 6.144 appears in the 10 percent interest column when ten payments are involved. Therefore, the implicit interest rate in this offer is 10 percent.

REFERENCE
APB Opinion No. 21, *Interest on Receivables and Payables* (1971).

INCOME
Income has been defined in various ways by authoritative sources:

1. "Income and profit... refer to amounts resulting from the deduction from revenues, or from operating revenues, of cost of goods sold, other expenses, and losses..." (Committee on Terminology, 1955).

2. "Net income (net loss)—the excess (deficit) of revenue over expenses for an accounting period..." (Accounting Principles Board, 1970).

3. "Comprehensive income is the change in equity (net assets) of an entity during a period of transactions and other events and circumstances from nonowner sources" (Financial Accounting Standards Board, 1980).

The measuring and reporting of income and its components are among the most significant accounting problems. Income as reported on the income statement can be conceptualized as follows:

Revenues – Expenses + Gains – Losses = Net income.

Income determination is based upon the matching of efforts (expenses and losses) and accomplishments (revenues and gains). Two approaches are available to compute net income: the net assets approach and the transaction approach. Under the net assets approach, the net assets (total assets – total liabilities) of an enterprise are compared at the beginning and ending of a period. If there have been no investments or withdrawals of assets by owners during the period, the increase in net assets represents net income. A decrease represents a net loss. The net assets approach to computing net income can be conceptualized as follows:

Net income = Ending net assets – Beginning net assets + Asset
withdrawals – Asset investments.

For example, assume that a company's net assets at the beginning of a period were $100,000 and at the ending, $150,000. Owners invested $10,000 and withdrew $5,000 during the period. Net income is computed as follows:

Ending net assets	$150,000
Deduct: Beginning net assets	100,000
Change in net assets during the period	50,000
Add: Asset withdrawals	5,000
	55,000
Deduct: Asset investments	10,000
Net income for the period	$ 45,000

The transaction approach measures income and reports revenues and expenses relating to the enterprise that result in net income. This information is especially useful for decision making. For example, the accounting records could provide the following information:

Revenues	$150,000
Deduct: Expenses	105,000
Net income	$ 45,000

The term *profit* is generally used to refer to an enterprise's successful performance during a period. Profit has no technical meaning in accounting and is not displayed in financial statements. The term has no significant relationship to income or comprehensive income. The term *gross profit* is sometimes used to indicate the excess of sales over cost of goods sold.

See also Income statement; Expense; Revenue.

REFERENCES
SFAC No. 3, *Elements of Financial Statements of Business Enterprises* (FASB, 1981).
SFAC No. 5, *Recognition and Measurement in Financial Statements of Business Enterprises* (FASB, 1984).

INCOME STATEMENT
An income statement presents the results of operations for a reporting period. The income statement provides information concerning return on investment, risk, financial flexibility, and operating capabilities. Return on investment is a measure of a firm's overall performance. Risk is the uncertainty associated with the future of the enterprise. Financial flexibility is the firm's ability to adapt to problems and opportunities. Operating capability relates to the firm's ability to maintain a given level of operations.

The question of how income should be reported on an income statement is an important accounting issue. Various theories have been used to suggest answers to this question. The current operating theory of net income emphasizes ordinary, normal, and recurring operations of the entity during the current period. Unusual or nonrecurring items (extraordinary items) and prior period adjustments (mainly accounting errors of prior periods) are excluded from the income statement and reported directly in the statement of retained earnings. Proponents of this theory maintain that the normal earnings represent what the enterprise is able to earn under current year's operating conditions and is the most useful figure for predicting future earnings. Excluding certain items from the income statement makes year-to-year comparisons more relevant.

The all-inclusive theory of income determination includes all revenues, gains, expenses, and losses affecting owners' equity during the period. According to this theory, extraordinary items and prior period adjustments are part of income. Proponents of this theory maintain that the annual income statements of the enterprise when added together should equal total net income for the firm during its existence. Such reporting provides a complete history of the earnings of the entity. Also, by excluding extraordinary items and prior period adjustments, management can manipulate annual earnings by choosing what to include or exclude from the statements.

The current official view expressed by the Accounting Principles Board is that income "should reflect all items of profit and loss recognized during the period," except for a few items that would go directly to retained earnings, notably prior period adjustments. The following summary illustrates the income statement currently considered to represent generally accepted accounting principles:

Revenues	$XXX
Deduct: Expenses	XXX
Gains and losses that are not extraordinary	XXX
Income from continuing operations (+ , –)	XXX
Discontinued operations (+ , –)	XXX
Extraordinary gains (+) and losses (–)	XXX
Net income	$XXX

Generally accepted accounting principles require disclosing earnings per share amounts on the income statement of all publicly reporting entities. Earnings per share data provides a measure of the enterprise's management and past performance and enables users of financial statements to evaluate future prospects of the enterprise and assess dividend distributions to shareholders. Disclosure of earnings per share effects of discontinued operations and extraordinary items is optional but is required for income from continuing operations, income before extraordinary items, the cumulative effect of a change in accounting principles, and net income.

See also Income; Revenue; Expense; Income taxes; Objectives of financial reporting.

REFERENCE

Welsch, Glenn A., Newman, D. Paul, and Zlatkovich, Charles T., *Intermediate Accounting* (Irwin, Homewood, IL, 1986).

INCOME TAXES

The Tax Reform Act of 1986 is the most sweeping federal tax legislation since the wartime Revenue Act of 1942. The 1986 act dramatically lowered marginal tax rates which will require many taxpayers to reorient their thinking about taxes when making decisions.

Income taxes can have a major impact on many business decisions: the form of business organization, financing methods, sale or exchange of capital assets, investment incentives, accounting methods, revenue recognition, pension funding, and others.

Companies should establish a framework for dealing with income taxes. The process should involve the following broad steps:

1. develop tax objective(s),

2. identify strategies available for accomplishing these objective(s), and

3. develop specific applications of these strategies.

Tax objectives for most companies include (1) permanent saving of tax dollars, (2) reduction of tax liabilities, and (3) deferring tax liabilities to some future period.

Basic strategies relating to effective income-tax policies include (1) the direct method, (2) avoidance of traps and pitfalls, and (3) tax evasion (an unacceptable strategy). The direct method requires that tax strategies be structured around income opportunities, expenditure opportunities, deferral opportunities, a timing approach, and a tax provision approach. These strategies and applications can be summarized as follows:

Objective	Strategies	Applications
	I. The Direct Method	
Avoiding taxes	1. income approach	Tax-free income; the dividends exclusion
Reducing taxes	2. expenditure approach	Deductions: R&D, charitable, and other expenditures
Deferring (postponing) taxes	3. deferral approach	Tax deferral arrangements; tax deferred investments
All of the above	4. timing approach	Postponing income; early payment of expenses; taking advantage of tax changes
All of the above	5. tax provision	tax credits; special tax rates
	II. Avoidance of Traps and Pitfalls	Knowledge of tax laws, regulations, and court decisions; advice of accountants and lawyers
	III. Tax Evasion (not acceptable)	Not reporting taxable income; claiming deductions not allowed

I

INCREMENTAL COST ANALYSIS

Incremental, or differential, costs are the differences in cost between two alternatives. Incremental cost analysis can be applied to most decisions that involve alternative courses of action where financial factors are involved. For example, incremental cost analysis is useful when determining the most profitable stage of production at which to sell a product, accepting or rejecting orders, make-or-buy decisions, increasing or abandoning operations, and capital budgeting decisions.

Incremental costs are usually variable or semivariable in nature. Variable costs increase or decrease as volume increases or decreases and in the same proportion. Semivariable, or mixed, costs increase or decrease as volume increases or decreases but not in the same proportion because they contain some fixed costs. Fixed costs can be included in incremental cost analysis when a change in capacity of the operation is anticipated.

To be useful for decision-making purposes, a cost must be a relevant cost. To be relevant, a cost must pertain to the future and must vary among alternatives being considered. Historical costs are irrelevant; amounts already invested are "sunk" costs and are ignored when assessing new investments. For example, when choosing between two pieces of equipment and the material costs required for each machine is the same, the material cost is irrelevant for decision-making purposes. Several cases will be developed to illustrate the application of incremental cost analysis.

Case 1. Replacement of equipment. A manager purchases a computer for $100,000 on January 1, 19X1. The cash cost of operating the computer for the next ten years is expected to be $50,000 per year. At the end of ten years, the computer will be worthless. On January 2, 19X1, a salesman for a competing computer firm offers to sell a computer that can handle the same work at a cash operating cost of only $25,000 per year. The second computer would cost $200,000 and would have an expected life of ten years with no salvage value at the end of that period. Maintenance and repair costs of $1,000 per year are expected for both machines. The manager learns that he can get a $10,000 trade-in for the computer he purchased on January 1.

Using incremental cost analysis, the manager prepares a schedule of the future costs that differ between the alternate courses of action (income tax considerations are ignored).

Relevant incremental costs	Cash Outflows Over 10 Years	
	Keep Computer	Replace Computer
Cash operating costs	$500,000	$250,000
Cash salvage value if traded today		(10,000)
Cost of new computer		200,000
Total relevant costs	$500,000	$440,000

The analysis shows that the company will obtain cash savings of $60,000 over the ten-year period if the equipment is replaced. The $60,000 difference in total costs between the two alternatives is called the incremental cost.

Case 2. The make-or-buy decision. A manufacturer purchases certain parts used in the production of radios. The firm has idle capacity sufficient to manufacture these parts. The estimated cost of material, labor, and variable overhead expenses required to manufacture the parts total $100,000. No other use of the idle facilities is feasible. The cost to purchase these items from outside sources totals $90,000. Should the firm make or buy the parts?

The cost to purchase from outsiders is lower than the variable cost of manufacturing the parts with the idle plant capacity. The fixed costs of the available plant capacity (rent, insurance, etc.) are sunk costs and are irrelevant to the decision. The parts should be purchased from outside sources.

Management would want to consider other factors in addition to cost considerations when making a make-or-buy decision. Working capital requirements may be changed, morale problems may develop, production schedules might be disrupted, or relations with suppliers or customers might be affected. These factors could affect the decision.

Case 3. Possibility of additional sales. A factory is operating at 90 percent of capacity (45,000 units). Fixed expense is $100,000; variable expense is $6 per unit. The product is currently selling for $10 per unit. A customer in a foreign country has offered to buy 5,000 additional units at $7 per unit. If the order is accepted, total expense per unit is $8 ($100,000 fixed plus $300,000 variable expense divided by 50,000 units). It would appear that the firm will lose money if it sells the 5,000 units at $7 per unit.

	Current Volume	Additional Order	Volume if Order Accepted
Sales			
Current (45,000 @ $10)	$450,000		$450,000
Additional (5,000 @ $7)		$35,000	35,000
Less variable costs (@ $6)	270,000	(30,000)	(300,000)
Contribution margin	$180,000	$ 5,000	$185,000

The additional order will add a total of $5,000 towards the net income of the firm. The $100,000 fixed costs are not relevant to this decision because they do not vary among the two alternatives.

See also Capital budgeting; Contribution margin analysis; Fixed and flexible budgets.

REFERENCE
Montgomery, A. Thomas, *Managerial Accounting Information* (Addison Wesley, Reading, MA, latest edition).

INFLATION
Inflation is a persistent increase in the price level. Inflation is primarily (1) demand-pull inflation or (2) cost-push inflation. Demand-pull inflation arises when the demand for goods and

services exceeds the available supply in the short run. This type of inflation frequently occurs in a fully employed economy which leads to competitive bidding for economic resources. Cost-push inflation usually begins with increased costs of factors of production (wages, material costs) or increased prices of consumer goods (wage-price spiral).

There are two types of price changes:

1. specific price levels: price changes of a specific commodity or item, such as a car or house; and

2. general price level: price changes of a group of goods and services

In a technical sense, inflation refers to changes in the general price level. When the general price level increases, the dollar loses purchasing power—the ability to purchase goods or services. The opposite situation is referred to as deflation. Holding monetary assets and liabilities during periods of inflation or deflation results in purchasing power gains or losses. Monetary items are assets and liabilities that are fixed in terms of current dollars and cannot fluctuate to compensate for the change in the general price level. Monetary assets include cash, receivables, and liabilities.

Changes in the general price level can affect, adversely or otherwise, almost every business decision. Changes in the general price level can affect organizational planning, controlling, and evaluating functions:

1. Is any of the budgeted or reported net income due to inflation?

2. Did the company lose or gain purchasing power from inflation due to holding monetary assets and liabilities?

3. How did inflation affect the financial statements during the period?

4. Were changes in the general price level taken into con-

sideration when budgets were prepared? when dividend policy was determined? when analyzing financial statements? when evaluating performance of investment centers? when selecting a source or method of financing?

A price index is used to measure changes in price levels. A price index is a series of numbers, one for each period, representing an average price of a group of goods and services, relative to the average price of the same group of goods and services at a base period. The Consumer Price Index for All Urban Consumers, published by the Bureau of Labor Statistics of the Department of Labor in Monthly Labor Review, is perhaps the most widely used price index.

Current cost information is needed to deal with changes in specific prices. Replacement costs are commonly used in current cost systems and for decisions involving specific prices.

REFERENCE
Welsch, Glenn A., Newman, D. Paul, and Zlatkovich, Charles T., *Intermediate Accounting* (Irwin, Homewood, IL, 1986).

INFORMATION
Information is defined as any perceived or recorded fact, opinion, or thought. Information theory deals with the structure and performance of coded information systems.

Data are facts and figures that are accepted as input to an information system which can be stored and processed. Information is typically obtained by direct observation, communication, or experimentation. Internal, business data are usually compiled from historical records, such as sales invoices, purchase orders, and payroll records. Information relates to the output of data processing that is useful to the person receiving it. Financial statements of a company represent significant financial information about a company.

Information is useful if it provides a basis for action, especially for predicting and evaluating. An information system is a network of interacting and interrelated elements that accumulates, processes, and communicates information for users in decision-making situations. These operations can be visualized as a data processing cycle involving inputs, processing, storage, and outputs (see Exhibit I-1).

Exhibit I–1
Management Information System

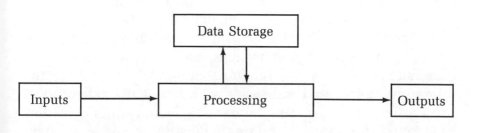

The value of information is determined by its relevance and reliability. Relevance refers to anything that would make a difference in a decision making situation. Reliability is a characteristic of information that refers to freedom from bias, verifiability, and faithful representation of what it purports to represent.

Information can be affected by noise and entropy. Noise refers to background activity which interferes with the information contents of a communication. Entropy refers to the fact that over a period of time the components of an information system (transmitter, processor, receiver) typically proceed toward sameness.

See also Information system.

REFERENCE
Moscove, Stephen A., and Simkin, Mark G., *Accounting Information Systems* (John Wiley & Sons, N.Y., 1984).

I

INFORMATION SYSTEMS

A management information system (MIS) is a process which organizes and communicates relevant information on a timely basis to enable management to perform its functions properly. The term *system* refers to the components or subsystems that interact and interrelate to accomplish a goal or objective. The activities of an information system include collection, processing, and communication of information. A management information system (MIS) includes the means by which information is provided to decision makers so that they may effectively attain the organization's goals and objectives. The major attributes of an MIS include the following: relevance, accuracy, timeliness, completeness, conciseness, economy, and flexibility. Subsystems of a typical business organization include the following: personnel subsystems, purchasing subsystems, production subsystems, marketing subsystems, order-processing subsystems, and financial subsystems. A primary subsystem is one that impacts the entire structure of an organization. A secondary subsystem is one that is limited to a single functional part of an organization.

Developing an MIS involves the following steps:

1. Establish the goals of the system.

2. Identify the information needed to attain the goal.

3. Design the system.

4. Test the system.

5. Implement the system.

6. Monitor and control the system.

These steps can be expanded in terms of (1) a feasibility assessment and (2) system design:

1. Feasibility assessment: preliminary analysis of current system; identification of reporting needs; requirements in terms of people, equipment, and forms; preliminary assessment of costs and benefits.

2. System design: complete description of the system; testing design to ensure that it can accomplish what it is supposed to accomplish.

A management accounting system should be designed to provide timely and accurate information to assist management develop product costs, control costs, improve productivity, increase efficiency and effectiveness, and motivate and evaluate performance. The system should serve as a communications channel between various levels of management, especially as they relate to (1) organizational goals and objectives and (2) product performance and production efficiencies. Sophisticated electronic technology is available to develop reporting and control systems that are accurate, timely, and effective.

A management information system should consider the benefits and the costs of information. The decision criterion for this concept is

Maximize Net Benefits = Benefits - Costs

The feasibility of the system and funds available to the organization for implementing the system are two constraints imposed on system design. Costs are defined as the cost (cash outflows and intangible costs) to be incurred to provide the desired information that would not otherwise be produced by the system. Such costs are considered discretionary system costs. System benefits include cash inflows and intangible benefits from reducing costs, increasing revenues, or changing the timing of cash receipts and disbursements. Outflows and inflows should be discounted when considered in the analysis.

Activities that constitute an internal accounting information system have been identified by the American Accounting Association's Committee on Concepts and Standards:

1. *Problem specification:* the structuring of the decision situation by the decision maker and his perception of a desire for information which will facilitate his choice of an action. It also includes the accountant's perception of the decision maker's decision model and information desires.

2. *Measurement:* the assignment of numbers to objects [when] the. . .purpose is to represent a given relation (or given relations) among subjects by the predetermined relation (or relations) among the numbers. Measurement is the accountant's task, one which consumes costly resources.

3. *Transmission:* the processing of data within the information system and communicating the information to users (decision makers). Both the process and the form of transmission are the accountant's responsibility and are potentially quite costly.

4. *Response:* the user's reaction (answer) to the messages transmitted by the information system. Once again the accountant's perception of this reaction is a significant determinant of system design.

Properties of information or information systems identified by the AAA's Committee on Concepts and Standards as the properties relate to the system activity are classified as follows:
Problem specification
  Relevance   Usefulness.

Measurement
  Accuracy   Precision and reliability.
  Consistency   Use of the same rules and procedures by the same company over time.
  Neutrality   Absence of bias.
  Objectivity   Supported by reliable evidence.

Precision	Used in describing the interval about a sample estimate.
Aggregation	Process of reducing the volume of data.
Verifiability	Information represents what it purports to represent; the method of measurement has been used without error or bias.
Comparability	Ability to bring together for the purpose of noting points of likeness or difference.
Uniformity	Not varying or changing; a function of comparability.
Flexibility	Potential of a system to support the planning and control processes.
Adaptability	Ability to which flexibility is made realizable.
Traceability	Audit trails.
Reliability	The chance that a confidence interval will contain the true value being estimated.

Transmission

| Timeliness | Having information available before its capacity to influence decisions is lost. |
| Aggregation | The process of reducing the volume of data. |

Response

| Understandability | The quality that enables users to perceive the significance of information. |
| Acceptability | Ability of user to recognize the presence of the desired data. |

Motivation	The attempt to achieve goal congruence between the goal of the respondent and the goal of the organization.
Fairness	Ability of being perceived as neutral.
Mutuality of objectives	Consistency of goals of those receiving information with the goals established by top management for the organization as a whole.

It is expected that trade-offs between various properties will be required in the design and implementation of any accounting information system.

See also Information; Cost accounting systems; Variances; Qualitative characteristics of accounting information.

REFERENCES
American Accounting Association, Committee on Concepts and Standards, *Report of the Committee on Concepts and Standards* (Sarasota, Florida, 1974).
Johnson, H. Thomas, and Kaplan, Robert S., *Relevance Lost: The Rise and Fall of Management Accounting* (Harvard Business School Press, 1986).
Maciariello, Joseph A., *Management Control Systems* (Prentice-Hall, Englewood Cliffs, NJ, 1984).
Wu, Frederick H., *Accounting Information System: Theory and Practice* (McGraw-Hill, NY, 1983).

INTERNAL CONTROL
Internal control refers to the systems, procedures, and policies employed by an enterprise to help assure that transactions are properly authorized and are appropriately executed and recorded. Internal control applies to both administrative controls and accounting controls. Administrative (operating)

controls include a plan of organization, procedures, and records that lead up to management's authorization of transactions. Accounting (financial) controls deal with the plans, procedures, and records required for safeguarding assets and producing reliable financial records.

Auditing standards require that accounting controls be designed to provide reasonable assurance that:

1. Transactions are executed in accordance with management's general or specific authorization.

2. Transactions are recorded as necessary (1) to permit preparation of financial statements in conformity with generally accepted accounting principles or any other criteria applicable to such statements and (2) to maintain accountability for assets.

3. Access to assets is permitted only in accordance with management's authorization.

4. The recorded accountability for assets is compared with the existing assets at reasonable intervals and appropriate action is taken with respect to any difference.

The major objectives of internal auditing control are to ensure the following broad administrative objectives:

1. The reliability and integrity of information.

2. Compliance with policies, plans, procedures, laws, and regulations.

3. The efficient and economical use of resources.

4. The safeguarding of assets.

5. The accomplishment of objectives and goals for programs and operations.

Administrative controls include most accounting controls but also extend to organizational plans, procedures, and records required to promote operational efficiency and adherence to management policies.

The system of internal control adopted by a company takes into consideration the size and nature of the enterprise. The establishment and maintenance of a system of internal control are the primary responsibility of management (and not of the auditor). The auditor evaluates control. The effectiveness of accounting controls depends to a great extent on the competence and integrity of an enterprise's personnel, their understanding of procedures, and the separation of assigned functions (e.g., no one person should handle all aspects of a transaction). To be effective, internal control procedures should assure that transactions are carried out with proper authorization and they are recorded at the amounts intended in the accounting periods in which they occur and are properly classified.

Broad categories of control procedures that apply to both financial and administrative controls include the following:

1. Organizational:
   a. Separation of duties.
   b. Clear lines of authority and responsibility.
   c. Formal policies.

2. Procedures:
   a. Accounting checks.
   b. Proper documents and records.
   c. Error detection and correction procedures.
   d. Physical control over assets and records.

3. Competent, trustworthy personnel (bonded where appropriate).

4. Performance goals and objectives:
   a. Periodic reviews of performance.

b. Comparisons of recorded accountability with assets.

5. Independent review of the system.

The Foreign Corrupt Practices Act passed in 1977 had a major impact on internal control applications in that it requires public companies to maintain reasonably complete and accurate financial records and a sufficient system of internal accounting controls. A major reason for this legislation was that Congress believed that public companies had inadequate controls to detect bribes and improper payments.

A review of internal accounting controls is essential to an audit of financial statements. A study of internal accounting controls enables the auditor to make a judgment concerning the reliance that can be placed on the records and for determining the nature, extent, and timing of various tests of the accounting data that the system has produced.

See also Fraud; Control function.

REFERENCE
Burton, John C., et al., eds., *Handbook of Accounting and Auditing* (Warren, Gorham & Lamont, Boston, 1981).

INVENTORY MODEL

The control of inventory involves two major considerations:

1. What is the optimal size for a purchase order?

2. When should the order be placed?

When considering the optimal order size, a manager knows that:

1. certain expenses tend to increase with an increase in order size, for example, storage-space cost, insurance, taxes, risk of spoilage or theft, interest on money invested to finance the inventory, etc.; and

2. other expenses tend to decrease with an increase in order size, for example, cost of clerical work associated with purchasing and receiving and paying bills, freight expense, etc.

As order size increases, the cost of ordering inventory decreases while the cost of carrying inventory increases. Exhibit I-2 illustrates the relationship between order size and inventory-handling costs. The optimal order size is the order size at which the ordering-cost and carrying-cost curves intersect. This relationship can be expressed in the following formula:

Economic order size = $\sqrt{2AP/S}$

where A = annual quantity used in units; P = cost of placing an order; and S = annual cost of carrying one unit in stock for one year. To illustrate this concept, assume that a company uses 3,600 units of inventory each year. The cost of placing an order is $8, and the cost to carry one unit in inventory for one year is $1:

Economic order size = $\sqrt{(2)(8)(3,600)/\$1}$

where A = 240 units.

The next issue to consider is when should inventory be ordered. If the lead time (the time between placing an order and receiving delivery), the economic order size, and the average usage are known, the time issue can be resolved. For example, in the illustration the demand is 3,600 units per year or approximately 10 units per day. One order of 240 units will last for about 24 days. The time between orders will have to be about 24 days. The order should be placed so that the new order will arrive just as the last one is used up. Suppose it takes 14 days from the time an order is placed until the goods arrive. In this case, each order should be placed 10 days after the last

Exhibit I–2
Economic Order Model for Inventory

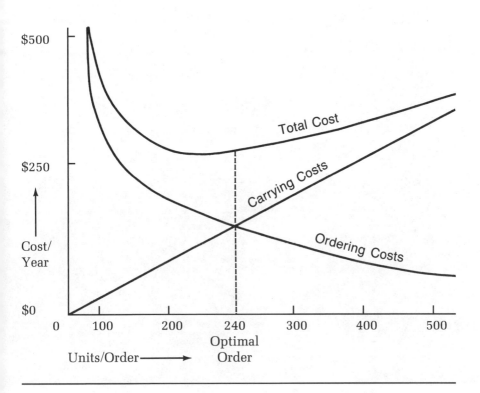

one has arrived, so that the new goods will arrive on the 24th day after the arrival of the previous order.

See also Planning function; Control function.

REFERENCE
Moscove, Stephen A., et al., *Cost Accounting* (Houghton Mifflin, Boston, 1985).
Tersin, R.J., *Principles of Inventory and Materials Management* (North-Holland, New York, 1983).

L

LEADERSHIP FUNCTION

Leadership is a major function of management. Basic functions of leadership include providing structure and ensuring motivation and compliance. Leadership is required if organizational goals and objectives are to be achieved. Leadership influences persons to act for a common objective. It is a quality of managers which involves getting subordinates (followers) to assist in the attainment of organizational ends. The skill of a leader relates to traits of the leader, the leader's knowledge of the personality, character, and needs/wants of followers, behavior patterns and interrelationships, situational dimensions (position power; task structure, leader-member relations), organizational requirements, and other factors. More specifically, successful leadership depends on:

1. the confidence subordinates have in their leader,

2. the nature of the subordinates' jobs, i.e., routine, non-routine, and

3. the authority or power placed in the leadership position, i.e., rewards and punishments.

L

To be successful, a leader should:

1. have expertise in the planning, organizing, and control functions of management, ˎ
2. have confidence in his/her ability to lead,
3. possess communication skills, and
4. should understand persons, tasks, organizational structure, motivation, personalities, the art of persuasion, etc.

Leadership theories are many and varied. Older forms of leadership theory are based on an understanding of the traits of a leader: maturity, character, decisiveness, intelligence, and others. Research generally confirms that no single trait or set of traits can assure effective leadership. Behavioral theories of leadership styles have been proposed to explain leadership. Behavioral theories include the following:

1. Autocratic vs. participative (democratic) styles
2. A "hands-on" management style
3. A two-dimensional model

The autocratic style of leadership is essentially leadership centered in the manager. The manager makes and announces the decision. The area of freedom for subordinates is limited and the use of authority by the manager is considerable. The participative leadership style is primarily subordinate centered leadership where subordinates have considerable freedom and the use of authority by the manager is limited. A "hands-on" management style requires a high degree of involvement in operations by a manager. Two-dimensional models of leadership are behavior-oriented. In two-dimensional models, one dimension focuses on people and the other dimension focuses on tasks (assignments; production). For example, a leadership style could be one in which the manager had a high concern for people and a low concern for tasks. Another style would be the opposite. A third style could be a moderate concern for people and tasks. A fourth could be high concern for both people and tasks. Other combinations are possible.

Leadership has been described by Robert Blake and Jane Mouton in The New Managerial Grid in terms of The Managerial Grid (see Exhibit L-1). The two-dimensional Grid identifies combinations of concern for production and concern for people. Concern for people is represented on the vertical axis of the grid; concern for production (tasks) represented on the horizontal axis. The four corners of the grid and the center describe various management styles:

Corner	Leadership Style
1,1	Low concern for both people and production.
1,9	High concern for people and low concern for production; democratic leadership.
9,1	High concern for production and low concern for people; autocratic leadership.
9,9	High concern for both people and production; Blake and Mouton believe that this style is the most effective leadership style.
5,5	Equal concern for people and production, i.e., a balanced approach to leadership.

See also Organizational behavior; Goals and objectives; Control function; Performance evaluation.

REFERENCE
Pennings, Johannes, M., ed., *Decision Making: An Organizational Behavior Approach* (Markus Wiener, New York, 1983).

L

Exhibit L-1
The Managerial Grid

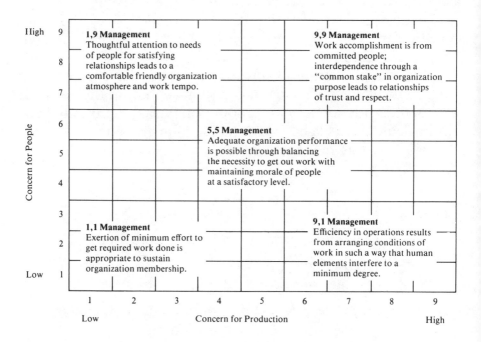

Source: Robert R. Blake and Jane S. Mouton, *The Managerial Grid*, Houston, Gulf Publishers.

LEARNING CURVE

A learning curve describes the relationship between direct labor hours per unit and cumulative units produced. When accumulated volume doubles, the labor hours per unit decreases by a constant percentage. An 80 percent learning curve indicates that when cumulative volume doubles, labor hours per unit are reduced by 20 percent to 80 percent of the previous level. As workers become familiar with a specific task, their productivity increases. This learning process is particularly noticeable in new products or processes. The learning curve was first used in World War II in the aircraft industry. The learning curve can be described algebraically as follows:

$$y(x) = ax - b$$

where y(x) = direct labor hours required to produce x unit

x = cumulative number of units produced

a = number of hours required to produce first unit

b = function the rate at which y(x) decreases as cumulative production increases

Edward L. Summers and Glenn A. Welsch in *Management Services* 7 (March/April 1970) listed activities most subject to learning curve analysis:

1. Activities which have not been performed or not performed in their present operational form.

2. Activities being performed by new employees and others not familiar with the operations.

3. Activities which involve the use of a stated raw material for the first time or which involve a change in the way the material is used.

4. Production runs of short duration, especially if these runs are repeated.

To illustrate an application of the learning curve, assume that a ship builder estimates that it takes 4,000 labor hours to produce a yacht. The company expected to build 8 yachts for various customers. The company estimates that its learning curve is 80 percent after the first yacht is built. The effect of the learning curve on labor hours is computed as follows:

Cumulative quantity	Cumulative average hours per yacht	Cumulative hours
A	B	C
1	4,000	4,000
2	3,200 (4,000 × .80)	6,400
4	2,560 (3,200 × .80)	10,240
8	2,048 (2,560 × .80)	16,384

Column A = Double the cumulative quantity.
Column B = Multiply the cumulative averages by the learning curve percentage.
Column C = Multiply the cumulative average by the cumulative quantity.

A learning curve chart is illustrated in Exhibit L-2.

Exhibit L-2
Learning Curve Chart

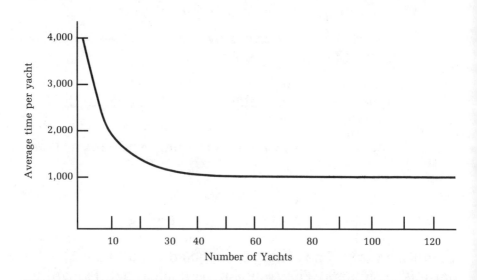

A firm that accumulates experience the fastest can benefit competitively over a long-run period. A knowledge of how the experience curve operates can help companies develop strategies for new products and processes, pricing, expansion, and other plans.

See also Pricing policy.

REFERENCE
Bufa, Elwood S., *Modern Production/Operations Management* (John Wiley & Sons, New York, 1983).

LEVERAGE

Leverage is used to explain a firm's ability to use fixed-cost assets or funds to magnify the returns to its owners. Leverage exists whenever a company has fixed costs. There are three types of leverage in financial management: operating, financial, and total leverage. Financial leverage is a financing technique that uses borrowed funds or preferred stock (items involving fixed financial costs) to improve the return on an equity investment. As long as a higher rate of return can be earned on assets than is paid for the capital used to acquire the assets, the rate of return to owners can be increased. This is referred to as positive financial leverage. Financial leverage is used in many business transactions, especially where real estate and financing by bonds or preferred stock instead of common stock are involved. Financial leverage is concerned with the relationship between the firm's earnings before interest and taxes (EBIT) and the earnings available to common stockholders or other owners. Financial leverage is often referred to as "trading on the equity." Operating leverage is based on the relationship between a firm's sales revenue and its earnings before interest and taxes. Operating leverage arises when an enterprise has a relatively large amount of fixed costs in its total costs. Total leverage reflects the impact of operating and financial leverage on the total risk of the firm (the

195

degree of uncertainty associated with the firm's ability to cover its fixed-payment obligations).

Financial leverage arises as a result of fixed financial charges related to the presence of bonds or preferred stock. Such charges do not vary with the firm's earnings before interest and taxes. The effect of financial leverage is that an increase in the firm's earnings before interest and taxes results in a greater than proportional increase in the firm's earnings per share. A decrease in the firm's earnings before interest and taxes results in a more than proportional decrease in the firm's earnings per share. The degree of financial leverage (DFL) can be measured by the following formula:

$$\text{Degree of financial leverage (DFL)} = \frac{\text{Percentage change in earnings per share}}{\text{Percentage change in earnings before interest and taxes}}$$

The degree of financial leverage indicates how large a change in earnings per share will result from a given percentage change in earnings before interest and taxes. Whenever the degree of financial leverage is greater than one, financial leverage exists. The higher this quotient, the larger the degree of financial leverage.

To illustrate the application of financial leverage, assume that an investor is considering the purchase of real estate with a selling price of $100,000. The investment will produce a net income of $15,000 annually. The investor has the option of acquiring the investment for cash or borrowed funds obtainable at the rate of 14 percent interest to leverage the investment. The effect of several leveraged options is illustrated in Exhibit L-3.

The example illustrates an investment where the financial leverage was positive. When the after-tax cost of borrowing exceeds the cash return that can be earned on the asset, negative financial leverage results. At this point, leverage cannot increase the rate of return to common stock equity.

Exhibit L-3
Financial Leverage

	Option 1	Option 2	Option 3
	Cash purchase (100% equity)	Leverage 1:1 (50% borrowed; 50% equity)	Leverage 4:1 (80% borrowed; 20% equity)
Acquisition price of asset	$100,000	$100,000	$100,000
Equity in investment	100,000	50,000	20,000
Income from investment before interest	15,000	15,000	15,000
Less: Interest on borrowed funds at 14%		(7,000)	(11,200)
Cash return	15,000	8,000	3,800
$\dfrac{\text{Cash return}}{\text{Equity investment}}$	$\dfrac{15,000}{100,000}=15\%$	$\dfrac{8,000}{50,000}=16\%$	$\dfrac{3,800}{20,000}=19\%$

Since debt financing incurs fixed interest charges, the ratio of debt to equity is considered a measure of financial leverage. This ratio indicates the relationship between the funds on which fixed financial charges must be paid and the total funds invested in the firm. The higher the debt to equity ratio, the higher the financial leverage and the greater the increase of operating profits and losses on earnings per share.

When an investor uses borrowed funds to acquire real estate or any other asset, any increase in property value belongs to the equity investor. The investor's equity increases substantially with only a modest increase in property value. To illustrate this concept, assume that an investor has an option to purchase real estate for $100,000 cash or by using 90 percent

197

financing. The investor holds the property for 10 years and the property increases at 4 percent per year. The percentage increase in equity growth differs dramatically when borrowed funds are used:

	Cash Purchase	90% Financing
Acquisition price	$100,000	$100,000
Equity investment	100,000	10,000
Investment value at end of 10 years	140,000	140,000
Percentage increase in equity growth:		
Equity growth		
Original equity	40%	400%

Operating leverage refers to the extent that fixed costs are utilized in the production process during an operating cycle. Operating leverage can also be used to measure the impact on earnings per share of having different levels of fixed to variable costs in manufacturing products. Earnings before interest and taxes are related to changes in the variable cost to fixed cost relationship. As fixed operating costs are added by the firm, the potential operating profits and losses are magnified, and are ultimately reflected in the variation in earnings per share of stock. For example, a book publisher's cost of producing another book is below the average cost of producing the book; hence, the gross margin (sales less cost of goods sold) per book is relatively large. An enterprise with a large percentage increase in income relative to its increase in unit sales can expect to have large operating leverage. The degree of operating leverage (DOP) can be measured by the following formula:

$$\text{Degree of operating leverage (DOP)} = \frac{\text{Percentage change in earnings before interest and taxes}}{\text{Percentage change in sales}}$$

The degree of operating leverage indicates how large a change in operating profit will result from a given percentage change in sales. As long as the degree of operating leverage is greater than one, there is positive operating leverage.

The degree of total or combined leverage (DTL) is computed as follows:

Degree of total leverage = Percentage change in earnings per share
(DTL) / Percentage change in sales

Whenever the percentage change in earnings per share resulting from a given percentage change in sales exceeds the percentage change in sales, total leverage is positive. The total or combined leverage for a company equals the *product* of the operating and financial leverages (DTL = DOL × DFL). Total leverage indicates a firm's ability to use both operating and financial fixed costs to magnify the effect of changes in sales on a firm's earnings per share.

Exhibit L-2 illustrates the application of leverages to a firm's income statement. In this illustration, note that fixed expenses and interest expense remain unchanged. Note the section of the statement involved in the computation of operating leverage, financial leverage, and total leverage. Also note that what provides the leverage is fixed expenses and interest expenses which remain unchanged. When operating, financial, and total leverages increase, the risks the firm assumes also increase since the total risk of the firm is related to the firm's ability to cover fixed operating and financial costs. In the illustration, note that the total or combined leverage of 2.0 is the result of multiplying 1.2 (DOL) by 1.67 (DFL). For this illustration, if sales increase by 1 percent, EBIT will increase by 1.2 percent. If EBIT increases by 10 percent, net income will increase by 16.7 percent. With total leverage of 2.0, to increase net income by 10 percent, sales must increase by 5 percent. Leverage analysis is an extension of break-even analysis and uses the same basic information: price, quantity, variable expenses, and fixed expenses.

See also Break-even analysis; Financial statement analysis; Ratios.

Exhibit L–4
Financial, Operating, and Total Leverage

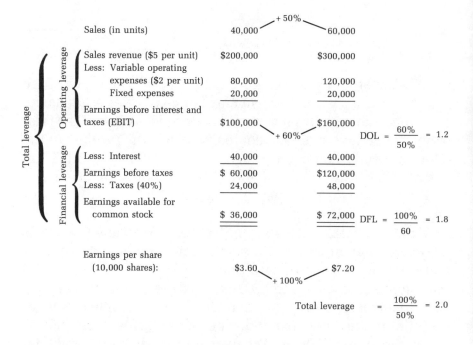

REFERENCES
Brigham, Eugene F., and Gapenski, Louis C., *Financial Management* (Dryden Press, Chicago, 1985).
Pringle, John J., and Harris, Robert S., *Essentials of Managerial Finance* (Scott, Foresman and Company, Glenview, IL, 1984).

LIQUIDITY

Liquidity describes the amount of time required to convert an asset into cash or pay a liability. For noncurrent assets, liquidity generally refers to marketability. Cash is a highly liquid asset. Property, plant, and equipment would ordinarily be very non-liquid assets. Liquidity is important in evaluating the timing of cash inflows and outflows. The liquidity of an enterprise is a major indicator of its ability to meet its debts when they mature.

Liquidity ratios are often used to measure a firm's liquidity. These ratios typically relate to the enterprise's working capital—its current assets and current liabilities. Current assets include cash, short-term marketable securities, receivables, inventories, and prepaid items. Current liabilities include such items as accounts payable, taxes, interest payable, and other such short-term payables. Major liquidity ratios include the current ratio and acid-test ratio computed as follows:

$$\text{Current ratio} = \frac{\text{Current assets}}{\text{Current liabilities}}$$

$$\text{Acid-test ratio} = \frac{\text{Quick assets}}{\text{Current liabilities}}$$

Quick assets include cash, short-term marketable securities, and accounts receivable. Inventories are excluded because there may be some delay in converting them into cash. Prepaid expenses are excluded because they cannot be converted into cash. The acid-test ratio is a more severe test of a company's short-term ability to pay its debts than is the current ratio.

See also Financial statement analysis; Ratios.

M

MANAGEMENT

Management is the process by which human efforts are coordinated and combined with other resources to accomplish organizational goals and objectives. Management has been defined as "the art of getting things done through people" (Mary Parker Follett). Management requires an understanding of (1) the economic principle of division of labor which breaks tasks down into subtasks and (2) the coordination of effort which reorganizes the subtasks in an efficient and effective whole.

Organizations which are managed have certain common characteristics:

1. individual effort is combined in pursuit of common goals and objectives,

2. tasks are divided in a meaningful way related to goal/objective attainment, and

3. power centers (hierarchy of authority) direct, review, and control effort.

A management function is a special duty or performance required of a person in the course of his/her work or position in a firm. Managers perform five basic functions: planning, organizing, directing, leading, and controlling. (See Exhibit M-1.)

Exhibit M–1
The Management Process

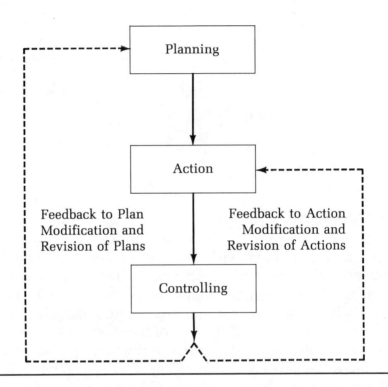

Planning is the means of coordinating an idea into a reality, i.e., determining the goals and objectives of the organization and the means of attaining them. Planning involves making decisions about a course of action and establishing priorities relating to the action.

Organizing and directing an enterprise requires that managers establish patterns of relationships (structures, hierarchies) among people and other resources that work to produce an output or accomplish a common goal or objective. Organizing and directing relate to the flow of work through the organization under guidance.

Leadership is required if organizational goals are to be achieved. Leadership influences persons to act for a common end or purpose. The skill of the leader relates to his/her knowing the personality, character, and wants of subordinates, behavior patterns, organizational requirements, and other factors.

Controlling is primarily taking appropriate actions to ensure that organizational goals and objectives are planned and carried out, i.e., that the firm attain maximum effectiveness.

Henri Fayol, the founder of the classical management school, identified fourteen principles of management:

1. *Division of labor.* Efficiency is improved when people specialize.

2. *Authority.* Managers give orders to get things done.

3. *Discipline.* Organizational discipline is required to achieve goals and objectives.

4. *Unity of command.* Each employee must receive instruction about a particular task from only one person.

5. *Unit of direction.* Operations that have the same objective should be under the direction of one manager.

6. *Subordination of individual interest to the common good.* The interest of the organization should take precedence over the interest of the individual.

7. *Renumeration.* Compensation for work performed must be fair.

8. *Centralization.* Decision making within organizations can be centralized or decentralized.

9. *Hierarchy of authority.* Authority in an organization should run from the top of the bottom.

10. *Order.* Individuals should be placed in the right position to be most effective.

11. *Equity.* Managers should treat subordinates fairly.

12. *Stability of staff.* High employee turnover is not efficient.

13. *Initative.* A degree of freedom should be given to subordinates to carry out organizational plans.

14. *Espirit de corps.* Team spirit gives a sense of unity to an organization.

Management by objectives (MBO) is a relatively recent innovation in management that often improves performance and morale. MBO involves managers and subordinates jointly establishing specific objectives and periodically reviewing performance to determine the progress that has been made toward attaining the objectives. MBO is based on the theory that people do find satisfaction in their work and will accept responsibility for their performance. To be effective MBO should have the approval and commitment of top management, provide for participation by subordinates in the setting of objectives, a degree of self-determination in implementing plans, and a periodic review of performance.

See also Planning function; Organizing function; Directing; Leadership; Control function; Information systems; Management theories.

MANAGEMENT THEORIES
Cultural values and technological developments are primary elements of most management theories. Several major theories include:

1. scientific management

2. classical organization theory

3. modern behavioral organization theory

4. information systems theory

5. quantitative management science

Modern management theory includes elements of each of these theories and, in that sense, can be considered eclectic.

Classical organization theory focused attention on the functions or processes of management. Some principles of management frequently associated with the classical theory include authority, discipline, unity of command, chain of command, unit of direction, centralization, order, and equity.

Scientific management had its origins with Frederick W. Taylor who applied principles of engineering to designing financial incentive systems to motivate workers. Time and motion studies were outgrowths of Taylor's scientific management theory. Such studies contributed to improvements in the utilization of human and natural resources, primarily at the shop level.

Modern behavioral organization theory focuses on human behavior: individual, group, organizational, and environmental. With the coming of the computer age, management theory began to deal with management information systems as they impacted on management practice and thought. Organizations are conceptualized as a set of interrelated systems, each with its set of inputs, processing, and outputs. How systems operate and how systems interface with each other and the external environment are major interests of information systems theories.

Quantitative management science focuses on decision making and uses economic effectiveness criteria measured in terms of costs as a major objective. Mathematical models and computers provide powerful analytical tools and techniques which are widely used in quantitative management science's approach to management.

In Search of Excellence, Peters and Waterman described eight attributes which characterized effective, innovative companies:

1. A bias for action

2. Closeness to the customer
3. Autonomy and entrepreneurship
4. Productivity through people
5. Hands-on, value driven
6. Remaining close to the business you know
7. Simple form, lean staff
8. Being both centralized and decentralized, i.e., loose-tight.

See also Management; Efficiency and effectiveness; Quantitative methods.

REFERENCE
Baker, Kenneth R., and Kropp, Dean H., *Management Science* (John Wiley & Sons, New York, 1985).

MEASUREMENT

Measurement is the assignment of numbers to objects, event or situations in accord with some rule or guideline. The property of the objects, events, or situations which determines the assignment of numbers is called the *measurable attribute* (or *magnitude*). The number assigned is called its measure (the amount of its magnitude). The rule or guideline defines both the magnitude and the measure.

In accounting, assets and liabilities currently reported in financial statements are measured by different attributes, depending on the nature of the item and the relevance and reliability of the attribute measured. Five different attributes of assets and liabilities are used in present accounting practice:

1. The historical cost of an asset is the amount of cash or its equivalent paid to acquire it. Historical cost for a liability is the historical proceeds received when the liability is incurred.

2. Current cost of an asset is the amount of cash or other consideration that would be required today to obtain the same asset or its equivalent. For liabilities, current proceeds is the amount that would be received today if the same obligation were incurred.

3. Current exit value is the amount of cash or its equivalent that would be received currently if an asset were sold under conditions of orderly liquidation. For liabilities, current exit value is the amount of cash that would have to be paid currently to eliminate the liability.

4. Expected exit value is the nondiscounted cash flow associated with the expected sale or conversion of an asset at some future date. For liabilities, expected exit value is the amount of cash expected to be paid to settle the liability in the due course of business.

5. Present value of expected cash flows is the cash flow associated with the expected sale or conversion of an asset at some future date discounted at an appropriate rate of interest. For liabilities, the discounted amount of cash expected to be paid to settle the liability in the due course of business.

Historical cost (or historical exchange price) method underlies the conventional accounting system. Inventories, property, plant, and equipment are often recorded at historical or acquisition cost. Current cost is also used in measuring inventories. Current exit value is usually used for marketable equity securities. Expected exit value is often used for accounts receivable and accounts payable. Present value of expected cash flows is frequently used for long-term receivables and payables.

The monetary unit of measurement used in current practice is nominal units of money, unadjusted for changes in purchasing power of money over time.

See also Accounting.

REFERENCES
SFAC No. 5, *Recognition and Measurement in Financial Statements of Business Enterprises* (FASB, 1984).
Staubus, George J., "An Induced Theory of Accounting Measurement" (Accounting Review, Vol. LX, No. 1, January 1985).

MOTIVATION

Motivation is an internal pressure which encourages, urges, or prompts a person or group to act or not act in a certain manner. Classical motivation theory relates to the concept that humans maximize their own self-interest. This conceptualization is reflected in Adam Smith's economic philosophy expressed in *The Wealth of Nations*. Humans are motivated primarily by economic concerns. Economics incentives in the industrial setting are under the control of the organization; employees are to be controlled and motivated by the organization. As rational-economic creatures, humans must not allow their emotions and feelings to interfere with economic activities, including motivation.

Advances on the classical theory suggested that basic human needs were the source of motivations and these needs were structured in a hierarchy: physiological satisfaction; safety and security; social needs; self-esteem and the respect of others; and self-actualization. The unsatisfied needs motivate human behavior. Individuals satisfy their lower level needs before proceeding to a higher level of need satisfaction which influences behavior. If a lower-level need is threatened, individuals will revert to that level.

Douglas McGregor developed the well-know theory of human behavior commonly referred to as Theory X and Theory Y. Individuals respond differently under the two theories of behavior. Theory X assumes a negative/passive approach to employees' motivation; Theory Y assumes a positive/active approach. Theory X of focuses on external direction and control factors. Theory Y focuses on integration and self-actualization as major behavior determinants. Theory X-type individuals dislike work, prefer directions, require control, and respond to threats; they are not ambitious, desire security above other needs, and are irresponsible. Theory Y-type people look for meaning in their work, possess initiative, are self-directing and problem-solving, and are committed to a job if it is satisfying; they are ambitious and seek responsibilities. According to many behaviorists, tasks could be structured to motivate, supervise, and direct people according to Theory X or Theory Y.

As might be expected, a Theory Z was proposed. William G. Ouchi undertook a study of the philosophy underlying Japanese business practice which concluded that Western businesses would probably be more successful, healthier, and happier work places if they adopted policies and practices found in Japanese industry. Qualities found desirable in Japanese organizations include lifetime employment, equality of worth, mutual respect, job flexibility, loyalty to the company, and nonspecialization. Ouchi proposed three types of organizations:

1. *Type J*: long-term employment, moderate evaluation and promotion policies, participative decision making, concern for the person.

2. *Type A*: tenuous employment, rapid evaluation and promotion, individual decision making, persons recognized as rational-economic creatures.

3. *Type Z*: a blend of Type J and Type A, placing considerable emphasis on trust, intimacy, and subtlety.

Frederick Herzberg proposed a Motivator-Hygiene Theory. Herzberg concluded that there were two sets of factors involved in work motivation:

1. Hygiene (or maintenance) factors—associated with job dissatisfaction

2. Motivator factors—associated with job satisfaction

A continuum of dissatisfaction-to-satisfaction exists. A degree of dissatisfaction is required to get people to work; as improvements are made in the hygiene factors, motivator factors can be employed to improve job satisfaction. Job enrichment and job enlargement programs when properly designed are strong motivator factors.

Henry A. Murray proposed another view of motivation in organizational behavior, a view that associated motivation with specific needs: the need for achievement; the need for affiliation; the need for power. Human motivation is dependent upon the strength of each need. Clayton P. Alderfer developed another need-related theory that associated organizational motivation with three categories of need: existence (physiological and safety-security needs); relatedness needs (social and esteem needs); and growth needs (self-actualization). These needs are arranged in a hierarchical order. When satisfaction exists, progression follows; when frustrated, regression follows.

Equity theories of motivation are based on two premises:

1. individuals expect something in exchange for their contribution to the organization;

2. individuals compare their contribution and rewards with those of others to determine if they are being treated equitabley.

Tension, stress, and dissatisfaction exist if individuals perceive themselves as being treated inequitably. Satisfaction follows when individuals perceive themselves as being treated equitably.

Victor Vroom proposed an expectancy theory of motivation that is based on the premise that the following conditions are met:

1. individuals believe that increased effort will result in increased performance;

2. they believe that increased performance will lead to a reward; and

3. they place a value on the reward.

The relationship between effort-performance and performance-reward are the basic elements of the expectancy theory of behavior.

Many additional motivationi theories exist and are beyond the scope of this survey.

See also Control function; Performance evaluation; Goals and objectives.

REFERENCE
Dessler, Gary, *Organization Theory: Integrating Structure and Behavior* (Prentice-Hall, Englewood Cliffs, NJ, 1985).

NEGOTIATING PROCESS

Negotiating is a basic form of decision making or social interaction. Negotiations typically involve:

1. several parties to the process,
2. potentially conflicting interests,
3. common interests and/or interdependencies, and
4. a degree of incentive to resolve an issue.

Many different and conflicting theories of negotiating exist. Most theories contain one or more of the strategies of organizational influence identified by David Kipnis and Stuart M. Schmidt:

Strategy	Behavior
Reason	This strategy involves the use of facts and data to support the development of a logical argument. Sample tactic: "I explained the reasons for my request."

Strategy	Behavior
Coalition	This strategy involves the mobilization of other people in the organization. Sample tactic: "I obtained the support of co-workers to back up my request."
Ingratiation	This strategy involves the use of impression management, flattery, and the creation of goodwill. Sample tactic: "I acted very humbly while making my request."
Bargaining	This strategy involves the use of negotiation through the exchange of benefits or favors. Sample tactic: "I offered an exchange (if you do this for me, I will do something for you)."
Assertiveness	This strategy involves the use of a direct and forceful approach. Sample tactic: "I demanded that he or she do what I requested."
Higher authority	This strategy involves gaining the support of higher levels in the organization to back-up requests. Sample tactic: "I obtained the informal support of higher-ups."
Sanctions	This strategy involves the use of organizationally derived rewards and punishments. Sample tactic: "I threatened to give him or her an unsatisfactory performance evaluation."

Source: Max H. Bazerman and Roy J. Lewicki, *Negotiating in Organizations*, (Sage Publications, Beverly Hills, 1983).

Success in negotiating involves many factors including the following:

1. Negotiate strategically, i.e., focus on corporate goals and objectives, and culture; external environment; ethical position.

2. Develop personal characteristics and skills, e.g., trust, coping, confrontation, assertiveness, stress handling capacity, leadership, interacting and interpersonal skills, exercise of power and authority, persuasive skills, logical reasoning, networking, and others.

Various approaches to collective bargaining situations include:

1. *Distributive bargaining:* involves the attainment of goals when they are in basic conflict with those of the other party; solutions usually result in a perception whcrc one person gains at the expense of the other.

2. *Integrative bargaining:* involves the attainment of objectives that are not in conflict with those of the other party; solutions can benefit both parties.

3. *Attitudinal structuring:* involves influencing the attitudes of another person, e.g., trust, friendship; solutions involve an improvement in attitude between the parties.

Negotiations typically proceed thorough three different stages:

Stage 1. Rules of procedures adopted; agenda identified; problems and issues identified.

Stage 2. Bargaining on problems and issues commences in earnest; positions are explored; settlement ranges established; conflicts arise; problems solved or found to be insoluble.

Stage 3. Closure and agreement.

Conventional wisdom maintains that persuasion is most effective when the following conditions exist:

1. Both sides of an issue are presented.

2. Negotiators understand that listeners remember the end of an argument better than the beginning; and the beginning and ending better than the middle.

3. Conclusions are stated explicitly.

4. To convince, create a need and then provide information about how that need can be satisfied.

5. In bargaining, emphasize the similarities of the positions instead of the differences.

6. Conflicting positions can be settled more easily if they are related to issues that have been settled or can be settled easily.

7. An advantage is obtained if one can determine an opponent's expectations and satisfaction level.

8. Knowledge and information can reduce risk and improve one's chances in negotiating.

9. Negotiating is easier if parties to the negotiating (1) have mutual respect for each other and (2) work to solve the other person's problems as well as their own.

10. Negotiating tactics which make high initial demands and avoid first concessions or make concessions slowly are more successful.

Research into traits of successful negotiators suggests that the following traits are important:

1. the ability to plan and prepare for negotiations,

2. the ability to reason clearly under stressful conditions,

3. the ability to listen carefully and express oneself clearly and persuasively, and

4. high self-esteem and personal integrity, and

5. high level of aspiration and expectation, high level of negotiating skills, and high level of perceived power.

Third-party negotiations are frequently arranged to help resolve organizational and personal conflicts. Psychological theories of conflict resolution, including interpersonal and intergroup training processes, are widely used.

See also Leadership; Communication function; Control function; Management.

REFERENCES
Bazerman, Max H., and Lewicki, Roy J., *Negotiating in Organizations* (Sage Publications, Beverly Hills, 1983).
Steers, Richard M., and Porter, Lyman W., *Motivation and Work Behavior* (McGraw-Hill, 1983).

NETWORK ANALYSIS

Various methods have been devised to plan and control a project having multiple steps or stages which are interdependent and sequential. Program Evaluation and Review Technique (PERT) is one such method. PERT was developed by the U.S. Navy Special Projects Office and was used to plan, schedule, and control the development of the Polaris submarine and other projects.

To employ PERT, it is necessary:

1. to list all the tasks (steps, activities) required by a project,

2. to arrange tasks in sequence, and

3. to estimate the time to perform each task.

For each task, an estimate of the time required to complete the task should be made:

1. an optimistic estimate: the shortest possible time required to complete the task,

2. a pessimistic estimate: the longest possible time required to complete the task, and

3. an estimate of what is considered most likely.

To illustrate PERT applications, assume that a warehouse is to be constructed according to the schedule shown in Exhibit N-1. A graph can be used to facilitate the analysis. In preparing PERT networks, each task can be shown as an arrow. The

223

expected time to complete each task is placed on the PERT network as shown in Exhibit N-2. The completion of a task (called
an event) can be shown as a circle.

Exhibit N-1
Construction Schedule for a Warehouse (in Months)

Activity	Expected time	Minimum time	Maximum time	Preceding activities
A Start planning	0	—	—	—
B Blueprints completed	3	2	3	A
C Site preparation	5	4	6	B
D Foundation laid	8	7	10	C
E First floor completed	9	10	12	D
F Storage area completed	8	10	12	D
G Inspection completed	1	1	2	A, B, C, D, E, F

Exhibit N-2
A PERT Network for the Construction of a Warehouse

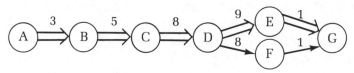

Critical path: 26 months shown by the double arrows

The next step is to identify the *critical path*, i.e., the longest
set of adjoining tasks through the network. In the illustration,
the critical path is A, B, C, D, E, G, which takes 26 months.
The critical path is shown as double arrows. Any delay in this
critical path delays the entire project. Delays along other paths
are not as important. The amount of time by which an activity

can be delayed without becoming a part of the critical path is called "slack." There is no slack along the critical path.

PERT can be modified to take into consideration any uncertainty in the time it takes for jobs in the project to be completed. PERT analysis can also be developed to include cost data. The estimated cost of a project is determined by summing the cost of each task. In certain cases, it may be possible to expedite the completion of a project (to earn a bonus or to meet a deadline) by reducing time required for a task along the critical path. The extra cost incurred in expediting the project can be compared to the original cost established to determine the cost of buying time in the critical path.

Once a PERT plan has been started, efforts should be made to maintain the time and cost schedules established for the project. Corrective action should be taken when needed to keep on schedule.

Critical path analysis has many advantages:

1. All activities are identified and planned.

2. Planning, performance, and control activities are coordinated (e.g., objective completion dates are established; potential bottlenecks are identified).

3. Scheduling is facilitated (e.g., the earliest and latest completion dates for network events can be specified).

4. Responsibilities and goals are established.

5. Project costs can be controlled and often reduced.

See also Planning Function; Control function; Decision making.

O

OBJECTIVES OF FINANCIAL REPORTING

The Financial Accounting Standards Board's Concepts Statement No. 1, *Objectives of Financial Reporting by Business Enterprises,* describes the broad purpose of financial reporting, including financial statements. The objectives in Statement No. 1 apply to general purpose external financial reporting and are directed toward the common interests of many users. The objectives arise primarily from the needs of external users who lack the authority to obtain the information they want and must rely on information management communicates to them. According to Statement No. 1, financial reporting should provide:

Information to help investors, creditors, and others assess the amounts, timing, and uncertainty of prospective net cash inflows to the related enterprise because their prospects for receiving cash from investments, from loans to, or from other participation in the enterprise depend significantly on its cash flow prospects.

Information about the economic resources of an enterprise, the claims to those resources (obligations of the enterprise to transfer resources to other entities and owners' equity), and the effects of transactions, events, and circumstances that change resources and claims to those resources.

O

Concepts Statement No. 1 also gives specific guidance about the kinds of information the financial reporting should provide:

Information about an enterprise's economic resources, obligations, and owners' equity.

Information about an enterprise's performance provided by measures of earnings and comprehensive income and their components measured by accrual accounting.

Information about how an enterprise obtains and spends cash, about its borrowing and repayment of borrowing, about its capital (equity) transactions, including cash dividends and other distributions of enterprise resources to owners, and about other factors that may affect an enterprise's liquidity or solvency.

Information about how management of an enterprise has discharged its stewardship responsibility to owners (stockholders) for the use of enterprise resources entrusted to it.

Statement No. 1 emphasizes that earnings information is the primary focus of financial reporting. According to this statement, earnings should be measured with accrual accounting. This requires that the financial effects of economic transactions, events, and circumstances should be reported in the period when they occur instead of when cash is received or paid.

The statement indicates that management is responsible for the custody and use of the entity's resources and that financial reporting should provide information concerning that stewardship function. Financial reporting also requires that reports should include management's explanations and interpretations that would be of benefit to external users in addition to quantitative information.

See also Accounting; Financial statement; Financial reporting; Financial accounting.

REFERENCE
SFAC No. 1, *Objectives of Financial Reporting by Business Enterprises* (FASB, 1978).

OPPORTUNITY COST ANALYSIS

Opportunity cost refers to the profit, or contribution, that is lost or forgone by using limited resources for a particular purpose. Opportunity costs arise from diverting an input factor from one use to another. Such costs do not require cash receipts or disbursements. Opportunity costs do not appear in the accounting records because they do not reflect a completed transaction.

Opportunity cost analysis is especially useful in evaluating alternatives. For example, there is an opportunity cost involved in using a machine to manufacture one product instead of another. To illustrate opportunity cost analysis, assume that a company can purchase some parts that it needs for production purposes for $10,000 from a supplier. It can make the parts for $8,000. However, if it makes the parts, it must use plant space that could be rented for $3,000. Opportunity cost analysis proceeds as follows:

	Make	Buy
Cost of obtaining parts	$ 8,000	$10,000
Opportunity cost: rental income lost	3,000	
Total	$11,000	$10,000

The company should purchase the parts from the outside supplier at a lower cost than it can make the parts when opportunity costs are considered.

Another illustration of the application of opportunity cost analysis can shed some additional light on the issue. Suppose that a staff accountant earning $25,000 a year has a job offer with a salary of $30,000. The job will last for one year. To take the job, the accountant would incur additional living cost of $6,000 for the year. In analyzing this decision, the accountant should consider the $25,000 salary forgone as an opportunity cost of taking the new job. This cost along with the additional living cost of $6,000 would not make the $30,000 job economically attractive. One should keep in mind that intangible costs and benefits could have an impact on the decision.

231

See also Incremental cost analysis; Break-even analysis; Contribution margin analysis; Gross margin analysis.

REFERENCE
Benston, George J., ed., *Contemporary Cost Accounting and Control* (Dickenson, Encino, CA, 1977).

ORGANIZATIONAL BEHAVIOR

Planning, control, budgeting, and pricing activities of management are influenced by and have influence on the behavior of people who work in the organization. There are many aspects of organizational behavior. Major areas of organizational behavior have been identified:

1. *Organizational theory and decision making.* This area deals with such matters as organizational structure (centralized/decentralized; functions of organizations; line and staff structures).

2. *Motivation and perception.* Human needs, levels of needs, and relationships.

3. *Communications.* Formal and informal communication structures and networks.

4. *Behavioral science.* Behavioral impacts of management and managerial activities.

5. *Ethical issues.* Competence, independence, integrity, and fairness (equity).

Behavior in organizations is conditioned by many factors including organizational structure, management styles, control systems, and others.

The way an organization is structured influences behavior. In an organization structured functionally, managers are assigned responsibility for a particular function(s), e.g., production, marketing. Such arrangements usually promote efficiencies by providing for specialization and economies of scale as the company increases in size. Profit-making responsibilities cannot be easily evaluated because profits result from the joint efforts of functional managers. Planning and coordinating production and marketing become more difficult and require coordination and cooperation. When organizations are structured along divisional lines, managers are given considerable autonomy and responsibility for functions usually assigned to an independent company. Each manager has responsibility for production, marketing, and profitability. Coordination of functions is easier to accomplish when functions are centralized in one position. Changes are usually easier to bring about.

The interactions of individuals and groups are coordinated and controlled by managers, i.e., the human side of the organization. As a result, management behavior can influence the behavior of the organization. How managers perceive the goals and objectives of the organization and how they respond to them can be affected by the managerial style the manager brings to the job. How managers motivate subordinates so that organizational goals and objectives are achieved can strongly influence behavior: rewards vs. punishments; behavioral vs. conceptualization approaches.

The nature and scope of controls imposed by managements influence organizational behavior. Controls are determined to a great extent by management's philosophy, the nature of the work involved, and the characteristics of the individual manager.

Modern organizational theory incorporates behavioral considerations into its underlying assumptions. Behavioral studies provide some preliminary insights in the area of control, especially with regard to procedures of setting standards:

1. Control systems that encourage responsibility by self-discipline rather than through unbending rules are often more effective within complex business environments.

2. Employees tend to develop their own standards and to manipulate norms established by management, especially when the norms are considered unreasonable or unfair.

3. Feedback on variances from standards tends to emphasize underachievement (unfavorable variances) and punishment, rather than overachievement and reward.

Behavioral studies relating to the budgeting process indicate that where conflicts arise over proposals for use of resources, each competing group sees its project as superior to those of competitors. In capital budgeting, goal achievement is a primary motivating factor. Failure to achieve a goal creates conflicts and influences behavior and attitudes negatively. Goal attainment or failure to attain a goal in one budget period affects behavior, attitude, and motivation in a subsequent period. When a group or individual has experienced success, subsequent action tends to improve; failure tends to lower levels of aspiration and achievement.

Behavioral studies also indicate that managers close to the sources of information can usually make better decisions than superiors who are remote from such information. Also, managers who can associate their responsibilities with what their responsibilities would be if they were acting for their own personal business, who can adopt an entrepreneurial attitude, frequently are more highly motivated. These findings tend to support a decentralized organizational structure as an attractive method of organizing an entity.

See also Motivation; Planning function; Control function; Performance evaluation; Budget; Centers; Goals and objectives; Responsibility accounting; Delegation; Pricing policy; Directing; Communication function; Management; Management theories; Organizing function; Controller; Ethics.

REFERENCES
Dressler, Gary, *Organization Theory* (Prentice-Hall, Englewood Cliffs, NJ, 1986).
Steers, Richard M., *Introduction to Organizational Behavior* (Scott, Foresman, Glenview, IL, 1984).

ORGANIZING FUNCTION

Organizing is a major function of management. The primary purpose of organization is to provide for the efficient and effective accomplishment of the goals and objectives of the enterprise. The goals and objectives established for an organization which are developed through the planning process serve as the basis of the organizing function.

Organizing an organization requires that managers establish patterns of relationships (structures, hierarchies) among people and other resources that work to produce an output or accomplish a common objective. Organizing is related to how work flows through the organization under guidance. It involves assigning responsibilities through the division of labor and the coordination of the parts into a cohesive whole. The coordination of effort requires the development of effective communications throughout the enterprise. Finally, organization requires the establishment of an authority structure that defines decision-making powers.

Organization theory has identified certain principles that can be used effectively in designing an organization structure:

1. *Specialization:* the tasks assigned to individuals should be limited.

2. *Objectivity:* activities and functions that are directed towards achieving an enterprise's goals and objectives are to be provided.

3. *Specification:* authority and responsibilities should be clearly communicated, preferably in writing.

4. *Authority and responsibility:* authority given should be commensurate (equal) to responsibilities assigned.

5. *Unity of command:* subordinates should have only one superior. Exceptions must be appropriately justified.

An enterprise can be organized in many different ways. It is helpful to identify the organizational structure of a firm through an organization chart. The organizational chart is a blueprint in the form of a pyramid which shows:

1. the command structure of the firm,

2. delegation of responsibilities,

3. relationships between units of the enterprise, and

4. formal channels of communication.

The organizational chart can also be designed to show line and staff relationships. Line positions involve persons who are directly associated with operations and who are directly responsible for creating and distributing the goods or services of the organization. Line authority is reflected by the typical chain of command that begins with the board of directors and extends down through various levels in the enterprise. Production and sales departments are examples of line activities. Staff refers to persons or groups in an enterprise whose major function is to provide advice and service to the line positions. Personnel and internal auditing departments are staff activities. Exhibit O-1 shows an organizational chart for a firm which has both line and staff positions. Observe that authority flows from top to bottom. No individual is subject to more than one person with respect to one task. These command relationships reduce or prevent confusion, inefficiencies, and frustration.

The preparation of an organization chart must take into consideration the span-of-control, or scope, principle which refers to the question of the size of each group or department of a firm, especially as it relates to the number of subordinates

---

Exhibit O–1
Line and Staff Relationships

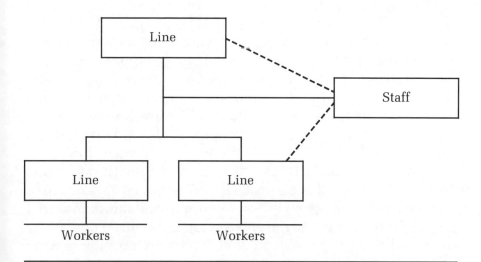

---

who report to a supervisor. The number of persons reporting to a supervisor is important because (1) it has an influence on the complexity of the jobs of individual managers, and (2) it determines the configuration of the enterprise (the fewer the number of people reporting to a supervisor, the more managers required). Some research indicates that the span of control for managers at the middle and top management positions varies from three to nine, depending upon the specific job (complexity or interdependency), job responsibilities, the manager's ability, the employees supervised, the rate of company growth, and similar factors. At the first-line manager's level, the span can be effective with as many as 30 subordinates.

In addition to the line-and-staff model, a collegial organization model is sometimes used as a method for organizing, especially where professionals (doctors, lawyers, academicians) are associated. In such situations, consensus among the members becomes the basic organizing factor.

O

In organizing an enterprise, consideration must be given as to whether authority should be centralized or decentralized. This issue refers primarily to the degree of control a person has over assigned job activities and responsibilities, a matter of depth. In a decentralized firm, decision-making authority is pushed downward through the organizational level to enable effective planning and operations at the most appropriate level. Decentralized operations enable the firm to meet its goals and objectives while providing autonomy to managers to enable them to test their ideas and skills, and to develop their potential. The extent to which a firm decentralizes its operations depends on the firm's environment (e.g., competition situation, market characteristics), the size and growth rate of the firm, and the firm's characteristics (e.g., costs and risks involved, top management's preferences, available managerial skills, and the history of the enterprise). Centralized operations are usually used by a firm that wants to provide greater uniformity of actions or integration of organizational effort.

An organization can be organized by:

1. function, e.g., marketing, finance, production;

2. process or technical operations, e.g., assembly, painting, drying;

3. product, e.g., cars, trucks, jeeps;

4. customer (wholesalers, retailers, direct sales); and

5. geography, e.g., Eastern, Western.

Management of an enterprise can be organized at various levels:

1. Top management—the chief policymakers of an enterprise whose primary managerial function is to coordinate the activities of the organization as a whole; top managers are accountable to owners and include the chairman of the board, the president, and other top organizational officers.

2. Middle management—supervisors of plants, divisions, departments, and other organizational units who stand as a link between top management and first-line management; middle managers interpret and execute company policy throughout the enterprise.

3. First-line management—foremen, section chiefs, and similar managers who spend most of their time with subordinates and who are responsible for the final execution of organization policy.

See also Planning function; Control function; Management; Organizational behavior; Centralization versus decentralization.

REFERENCE

Dressler, Gary, *Organization Theory* (Prentice-Hall, Englewood Cliffs, NJ, 1986).

Pfeffer, Jeffery, *Organizations and Organization Theory* (Pittman, Belmont, CA, 1982).

PERFORMANCE EVALUATION

Performance evaluation is based upon the application of guidelines against which the organization's efforts and accomplishments can be measured. Evaluation implies the existence of a benchmark against which actual performance can be compared. Evaluation can result in the identification of both successes and failures. Comparing actual performance with standard performance is commonly referred to as feedback. Feedback provides a basis for interpreting the results of the evaluation and reinforces the successes and eliminates the failures.

Performance evaluation of profit centers typically focuses upon (1) net income or (2) contribution toward the firm's income. Performance evaluation usually reflects this relationship:

$$\text{Operation ratio} = \frac{\text{Income}}{\text{Sales}}$$

Performance evaluation of an investment center typically focuses on (1) the return on investment (ROI) and (2) residual income. ROI is conceptualized as follows:

243

$$\text{ROI} = \frac{\text{Income}}{\text{Investment (or Capital employed)}}$$

The residual income approach charges an investment center with an interest charge for the assets employed. The interest charge is usually the company's cost of capital. Performance is evaluated in terms of income earned in excess of the minimum desired rate of return:

Residual income = Investment center income − Interest charge

See also Organizational behavior; Control function; Communication function; Goals and objectives; Leadership function; Motivation; Segment performance; Return-on-investment analysis; Ratios; Centers; Responsibility accounting.

REFERENCE
Daft, Richard L., *Organization Theory and Design* (West, St. Paul, MN, 1983).

PLANNING FUNCTION
Planning is a major function of management. Planning is a process that (1) establishes goals and objectives, and (2) develops a decision model for selecting the means of attaining those goals and objectives.

The strategic planning model consists of four components:

1. Basic research and analysis of internal and external environments and identification of macro- and micro-level trends.

2. Identification and analysis of alternative goals and objectives.

3. Statement of goals and objectives.

4. Development of policy alternatives and resource utilization.

The goal of a profit-making organization is typically to maximize the profit of the business. One of the decision models for implementing that plan might be the preparation of a budget for the coming year.

Planning requires that an organization make choices relating to:

1. goals and objectives, or what you want to do and why you want to do it, and

2. the means of attaining these ends, or when, where, and how to do it.

By definition, goals and objectives must be predetermined; they must be set in advance of activities undertaken to achieve them. Goals can be either general or specific. General goals are typically long-term goals. Specific goals, sometimes referred to as objectives or intermediate goals, are usually, but not always, short-term. Goals provide the incentives as well as the rewards for what one does.

Three types of planning are basic to goal realization:

1. strategic planning (a business plan),

2. short-run planning (forecasting and budgeting), and

3. project and situation planning

Strategic planning involves establishing the basic philosophy and direction of the organization as well as the strategic decisions necessary for achieving the goals of the organization. It requires making decisions and setting policies such as the following:

1. Are you in the right business?

2. In addition to maximizing profit, what other objectives do you have for the organization? For example, the organization may have additional objectives including market position, productivity, product leadership, service to customers, and others.

3. What manufacturing and/or marketing methods should be used?

4. What financing sources should be relied on?

Short-run planning involves deciding how the organization will utilize the available resources during a period of time (usually one year or less). Short-run planning identifies the results the organization expects to achieve during this time frame. Short-run planning is often reflected in forecasts and budgets.

Project and situation planning involve decision making that relates to specific projects or situations. For example, the acquisition of equipment to replace an existing one, the discontinuance of a particular department or division of the company. Project and situation decisions involve specific actions that usually have long-run implications for the company.

A hierarchy of planning showing types of planning, levels, and scope can be conceptualized as follows:

Type	Level	Scope
Goals and objectives of the organization	Top management	Broad, company wide, and long-term
Policies, departmental	Middle management	Narrow, variable terms, tactical, flexible
Procedures and methods	Line and supervisory	Narrow, variable terms, detailed

See also Control function; Motivation; Communication function; Leadership function; Organizing function; Pricing policy; Management; Management theories; Goals and objectives; Decision making; Organizational behavior; Performance evaluation; Network analysis.

REFERENCES
Fallon, William K., ed., *AMA Management Handbook* (AMACOM, New York, New York, 1983).
Parson, M. J., *Back to Basics Planning* (Facts on File Publications, New York, 1985).
Reinharth, L.; Shapiro, H.; and Kallman, E., *Planning: Strategic, Administrative, Operational* (Van Nostrand Reinhold, Florence, KY, 1980).

PRICING POLICY

Pricing is a profit-planning situation in which management searches for alternative pricing policies and evaluates the profit consequences of the various alternatives before reaching a decision. Pricing policy refers to the principles and practices which determine pricing decisions. Theory and practice vary widely where pricing policies are determined, even within the same industry. Practices range from rule-of-thumb judgments, conventional practices, to microeconomic theory.

The establishment of a pricing policy is the product of organizational goals, objectives, strategy, and tactics. Pricing strategy has been defined as the art of projecting and directing the larger pricing issues within a marketing campaign in the longer term while ignoring short-term fluctuations in market or trading conditions. Pricing tactics refer primarily to manipulating prices to achieve short-term objectives.

Many factors are involved in the pricing decision including:

1. *Organizational goals and objectives.* Goals and objectives are said to be almost synonymous with pricing objectives. Pricing objectives, or targets, as related to overall organizational objectives typically refer to:

   a. a rate-of-return objective,

   b. a profit maximization objective, and

   c. nonfinancial objective(s), e.g., growth, market share.

2. *Costs.* Pricing theorists maintain that the primary purpose of using costs in pricing is to forecast the impact on profit of alternative prices. Costs usually set a minimum limit to price. Costs play a special role in special situations: product tailoring where the seller cannot affect the market price and so must adjust costs to make a profit; refusal pricing, where a product is designed for a single buyer; where a producer has a single buyer and the seller must price the product to prevent the buyer from making the product; and public utility pricing. Costs for pricing purposes should have the following characteristics:

   a. Costs should be expressed in terms of product or service units.

   b. Manufacturing and nonmanufacturing costs are equally important in pricing decisions.

   c. Current or future costs are required for pricing; historical or standard costs are useful as guidelines.

3. *Consumer demand.* Consumer demand is of major significance in establishing prices. Consumer demand is influenced by product differentiation and price elasticity.

4. *The market.* The market situation plays a major role in pricing decision. Prices are affected in different ways by competition, monopoly, monopolistic competition, and oligopoly.

5. *Legal requirements.* The government through laws, regulations, and commissions can have an impact on the pricing decision.

6. *Social and ethical responsibility.* Organizations should and often do take the impact of their pricing decisions upon society into consideration.

Specific economic, accounting, and statistical techniques have been developed to deal with pricing. The economic approach attempts to maximize profits by establishing a price at which marginal revenue equals marginal costs. This approach is discussed in this book under the entry Pricing policy: economic theory. Accounting approaches to pricing usually relate to some form of cost-plus pricing. Many entries in this book under Pricing policy describe various forms of cost-plus pricing. Sophisticated statistical approaches to pricing have also been developed and used in business. Statistical approaches rely heavily on probability theory which assesses the probabilities of events that determine the profitability of alternative actions available to the decision maker.

Marketing theorists generally agree that the pricing process involves:

1. identifying markets to be targeted,

2. constructing the marketing mix,

3. selecting a pricing policy or objective(s),

4. determining price strategy and tactics, and

5. establishing the specific price.

Pricing products and services is primarily a function of what the market will pay. What the market will pay is a function of the nature of the market, the competition, design and quality of the product or service, the company's positioning in the market, and the life cycle of the product or service. Basic pricing strategies include the following:

1. low pricing to limit competition and protect market share,

2. let competition or a market leader establish the price,

3. be below the market to provide a competitive edge, and

4. price what the market will bear.

When setting the final price for a good or service, management typically uses one of the four following methods:

1. *Demand-based methods:*

   a. Skimming: a high initial price customers are willing to pay for a new or innovative product that customers want.

   b. Penetration: low initial price to discourage competition.

   c. Prestige: high price to attract status-conscious customers.

   d. Price lining: a line of products may be priced at a number of different specific pricing points (a price lining).

   e. Odd-even pricing: pricing a product a few dollars or cents under an even number, e.g., $99.99.

   f. Demand-backward pricing: estimate the price that consumers would be willing to pay; work backward through margins and costs that will have to paid to retailers and wholesalers and costs incurred to establish the price to be charged wholesalers.

2. *Cost-based methods:*

   a. Markup pricing: add a fixed percentage to the cost of an item(s).

   b. Cost plus percentage of cost: add a fixed percentage to production or construction cost.

   c. Cost plus fixed-fee pricing: Supplier is to be reimbursed for cost plus a fixed fee.

   d. Experience curve: the cost of many products and services declines each time a firm gains experience or learns how to produce and market the product or service. Pricing of products or services would take this experience into consideration when pricing. For example, if a firm estimates that costs will fall by 30 percent each time volume doubles, the cost for the 100th unit produced and sold will be about 70 percent of the 50th unit produced and sold; the cost of the 200th unit produced and sold will be about 70 percent of the 100th unit.

3. *Profit-based methods*:

   a. Target profit pricing: If variable cost per unit is $10, fixed cost is $100,000, volume of 1,000 units, and a target profit of $5,000, the price is computed as follows where:

   PRICE = P:
   Profit = Total revenue − Total cost
   $5,000 = (P × 1,000) − [$10,000 fixed + (1,000 units × $10)]
   P = $25 per unit.

   b. Target return-on-sales pricing: The following formula can be used to determine the price using the data from the previous illustration but desires a 10 percent return on sales:

$$\text{Target return on sales} = \frac{\text{Target profit}}{\text{Total revenue}}$$

$$10\% = \frac{\text{Price} \times \text{Quantity} - [\text{Fixed} + (\text{unit variable cost} \times \text{quantity})]}{\text{Total revenue}}$$

$$10\% = \frac{P \times 1{,}000 - [\$10{,}000 + (\$10 \times 1{,}000)]}{P \times 1{,}000}$$

   P = $22.20

   c. Target return-on-investment pricing: Assume an investment of $100,000 on which a company wants to make a 5% profit; the company expects to sell 1,000 units; fixed costs are $10,000 and variable costs are $10 per unit. The problem would now be solved using the procedure shown in "target profit pricing".

P

4. *Competition-based methods:* Competition based methods of pricing include (1) pricing at, above, or below the market, (2) loss leader pricing, (3) sealed bid pricing, and others.

Marketing formulas are available for calculating the selling price based upon (1) markup based on cost and (2) markup based on selling price:

1. Markup based on cost formula:
   Selling price = Cost (1 + Markup based on cost)
   Example: Policy is to mark up merchandise at 66⅔% of cost. If pants costs $12, the selling price is $20:
   Selling price = $12(1 + .66⅔)
   = $20

2. Markup based on selling price formula:
   $$\text{Selling price} = \frac{\text{Cost}}{1 - \text{Markup based on selling price}}$$
   Example: Policy is to mark up merchandise at 40% of selling price. If a product costs $240, the selling price is $400:
   $$\text{Selling price} = \frac{\$240}{1 - .40}$$
   = $400

See Free enterprise system; Goals and objectives; Experience curve; All following entries under *Pricing policy.*

REFERENCE
Benston, George J., ed., *Contemporary Cost Accounting and Control* (Dickenson, Encino, CA, 1977).

PRICING POLICY: ADMINISTERED PRICING

Administered pricing is a pricing policy in which a seller can exert an influence on the price charged for a product or service because of the absence of competition. Large and powerful producers are occasionally in a position to adopt administered pricing.

See also Pricing policy.

PRICING POLICY: CONVERSION COST PRICING

Conversion costs include direct labor and factory overhead costs. Costs of materials used in the product are not considered. Conversion costing is occasionally used when a customer provides the material. Conversion cost pricing requires that factory capacity is limited in terms of labor and overhead cost constraints. When conversion cost pricing is followed, companies direct their efforts to products or services requiring less labor and overhead (scarce resources) because more units can be produced and sold. For example, assume the following information:

	Product X	Product Y
Direct material	$10	$10
Conversion costs:		
Direct labor	5	1
Factory overhead	9	4
Total production cost	$24	$15

If the firm desires a 10 percent markup on conversion cost, the sales price for each product is:

	Product X	Product Y
Full cost	$24.00	$15.00
Markup on conversion cost:		
10% × $14	1.40	
10% × $5		.50
Sales price	$25.40	$15.50

More units of product Y can be produced because Product Y requires less conversion cost. Each product produces the same profit per unit of scarce resource.

See also Pricing policy; Planning function; Budget.

PRICING POLICY: COST-PLUS PRICING

Cost-plus pricing requires a firm to add a markup to an established or known average cost. The size of the markup depends upon what the firm calculates it can obtain. This form of pricing usually establishes a target rate of return on its investment and uses this rate to establish prices. Cost-plus pricing generally does not take into consideration the elasticity of demand or the relationship of marginal cost to marginal revenue. As a result, the price established may not be the most profitable price attainable. Costs should be used in pricing primarily to forecast the impact on profits of alternative pricing policies. Cost usually refers to full costs. Cost-plus pricing is in essence a backward-cost pricing method. A desired percentage for profit is added to the full cost of the product or service to establish the price. Highway construction, defense, and housing contracts frequently use cost-plus pricing methods. Cost-plus pricing usually involves the difficult task of allocating fixed costs which cannot be traced directly to a project.

A problem with full-cost pricing occurs when two or more products or projects are produced or worked on. How should common costs be allocated to the products or projects and how large should the markup be? In spite of these and other problems, full-cost pricing is widely used because (1) the economic model of pricing is difficult to apply, (2) managers consider full-cost pricing to be safe, and (3) intuitively managers believe that in the long run all costs, fixed and variable, must be recovered if the firm is to survive. However, full-cost pricing cannot guarantee any of these assumptions.

See also Pricing policy.

PRICING POLICY: DIFFERENTIAL COST PRICING

A differential cost is the increase in total costs resulting from the production of additional unit(s). A desired markup based as a percentage of differential cost is added to full cost. Differential cost pricing focuses on the contribution to fixed costs and profit that an additional order will produce.

See also Pricing policy.

PRICING POLICY: DIRECT COST PRICING

Direct costs include the direct cost of material and labor along with variable factory overhead costs. When direct cost pricing is used, selling prices are set at a percentage above these direct costs incurred in manufacturing or producing the good or service. Direct cost pricing is valid if the cost characteristics of a company's product lines are similar. If the indirect costs that should be allocated to each product line are not essentially the same percentage of direct costs, and if the assets employed by product lines are not similar, direct cost pricing can produce inequities in the pricing process. This method does not base pricing on indirect costs which are often arbitrarily allocated to products.

See also Pricing policy.

PRICING POLICY: DISCOUNTS

A discount is a reduction of a stated price. Major types of discounts include quantity, trade, cash, and seasonal discounts. Other discounts are based on geographical factors (zonal pricing based on delivery distance); delivery methods (discounts for customer collection); trade-in allowances on old equipment. Discount can be based on physical volume or dollar sales; a percentage discount or a cash difference from a list price; a flat sum rebate or a net price. Discounts can also be published, discretionary, negotiated, or a combination thereof. Major types of discounts and the reasons for using them are outlined here:

Type	Method	Objective
Quantity discount	1. Single order: based on volume purchased at one time.	Relates to individual customer. Encourage large orders. Pass on cost savings and economies in large orders.

Type	Method	Objective
	2. Cumulative: based on volume purchased over a fixed period of time.	Discourage small orders. Encourage repeat orders.
Trade discount	Percentage discount from a specific list price which supposedly represents distributors' expenses and profit. Trade discounts may be expressed as a flat rate or combined with a quantity discount.	Assists in controlling final selling price. Provides for discriminating between different types of distributors, e.g., retailers, wholesalers. Eliminates need to change catalogues, since discounts can be changed, not list prices.
Cash discount	Deductions offered by seller if payment is made within a specific time period.	Encourage early payment of account, reducing credit and collection risks.
Seasonal discount	Different prices depending on the season, day of week, or time of day where demand has a cyclical pattern and supply is fixed.	Encourage spreading of demand, avoidance of peak loading, and increasing demand during low periods, e.g., hotels, cinemas, and electricity.

See also Pricing policy.

PRICING POLICY: ECONOMIC THEORY

Pricing policies refer to the process of establishing the price of a company's product or services as well as the decisions relating to discounts to be offered and under what terms.

Major factors affecting the determination of a pricing policy include a consideration of:

1. the environment in which the product or service is sold,

2. the characteristics of the product or service,

3. the competition and other market considerations,

4. consumer behavior, and

5. government regulations.

Demand for goods and services. Demand for goods and services refers to the quantity that will be purchased at various prices at a given time. Demand is a function of price, income available for spending, prices of other commodities, and personal tastes. In general, the higher the price of a good or service, the less the quantity of the item people or firms will purchase. As prices rise, demand tends to fall off because (1) users of the product or service switch to substitutes and (2) present consumers reduce the consumption of most products. The lower the price, the more units of the product or service that will be demanded. When graphically presented, a demand curve appears with a downward slope (see Exhibit P-1).

Exhibit P–1
A Demand Curve

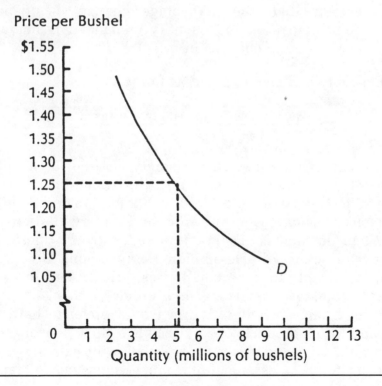

An increase in demand occurs when additional quantities of a product can be sold at the same price. A change in price alone can also change the quantity of a product demanded.

Price Elasticity of Demand. The impact of price changes on demand depends upon the price elasticity of a product or service. Price elasticity describes whether a given change in price will have a large, small, or no effect on demand. Price elasticity is described in terms of:

1. Unit elasticity: the percentage change in price is equal to the percentage change in quantity demanded.

2. Elastic demand: the percentage change in price is less than the percentage change in quantity demanded (i.e., quantity demanded is responsive to changes in price).

3. Inelastic demand: the percentage change in price is greater than the percentage change in quantity demanded (i.e., the quantity demanded is not very responsive to changes in price).

Elasticity can be computed as follows:

$$\frac{\text{Percent change in quantity demanded}}{\text{Percent change in price}}$$

If the coefficient of demand elasticity is larger than 1, the demand is elastic; if smaller than 1, the demand is inelastic; if equal to 1, the demand is unitary. Exhibit P-2 describes the characteristics of elastic, inelastic, and unitary elasticity.

When demand is elastic and a seller lowers (increases) prices, the seller will take in more (less) revenue. If demand is inelastic and the seller cuts (raises) prices, the firm takes in less (more) revenue. If demand is unitary, a change in price will not change revenue. A firm would prefer to have the demand for its products or services inelastic at a level above its current price and elastic at levels below its existing price. In such circumstances, the firm would gain revenue if it raised or lowered prices.

Exhibit P-2
Characteristics of Elastic, Inelastic, and Unitary Elasticity

Type	Effect on quantity demanded	Effect on total revenue as demand increases	Examples of products	Schedule		Graph
Inelastic	Quantity change proportionately less than price change.	Decrease	Necessities and products difficult to find substitutes; bread; eyeglasses	Price $10 9 8 7	Quantity 100 101 102 102.5	Demand for bread
Elastic	Quantity change proportionately larger than price change.	Increase	Luxuries and products for which there are many substitutes: travel abroad; TV sets.	$10 9 8 7	100 125 160 250	Demand for color TV sets
Unitary elasticity	Quantity change in exact proportion to price change.	No change	No good substitutes; one use for product	$10 9 8 7	100 111⅑ 125 143	Note that the demand curve of unit elasticity is not a straight line
Total inelastic	Quantity demanded is unchanged in spite of change in price.	Unchanged	Table salt and sugar	$10 9 8 7	100 100 100 100	Demand for table salt
Total elastic	Quantity demanded at an established price is infinite.	Infinite	Wheat, corn and certain other farm products	$10 9 8 7	Infinite Infinite Infinite Infinite	Demand for one farmer's output

Substitutes and Complements. If two products are substitutes for each other, the change in the prices of the substitutes changes the position of the demand curves. If the price of a substitute rises (falls), the demand for the other product rises (falls). For example, meat and eggs are substitute products. The ease or difficulty of substituting one product for another is a major reason for the degree of elasticities of goods and services.

If two products are complements, the products are so related that one cannot usually use one without the other. For example, automobiles and gasoline are complementary products; camera and film are complementary products. Complements are the opposite of substitutes. The degree that products are complementary is also a cause of elasticity.

Price and Output Within the Market. The cost of production side of a firm can be combined with the demand side to determine the price and output of a commodity or service in the market place. A firm behaves differently under conditions of perfect competition, monopoly, monopolistic competition, and oligopoly.

A market is perfectly competitive if:

1. there are a large number of sellers and buyers of a commodity where each is too small to influence the price of the commodity,

2. the outputs of all firms in the market are standardized, and

3. freedom of entry into and exit from the market by producers exists.

Monopoly refers to a type of market organization in which there is one producer of a commodity or service for which there are no close substitutes. Entry of more producers into the market is not possible.

Monopolistic competition, or imperfect competition, refers to a type of market organization in which there are many firms selling closely related but not identical products or services. Entry of new producers into the market is possible.

Oligopoly is a type of market organization in which there are few producers of a product which is somewhat standardized. The actions of each seller will affect the other sellers. The reaction of one firm to the action of another is usually indeterminate.

Exhibit P-3 summarizes the major characteristics of various market situations.

Before pricing under various market situations is discussed, it is necessary to define economic cost and revenue concepts:

1. *Total cost* (TC) is the sum of total fixed and total variable costs at a particular level of production.

2. *Average total cost* (ATC) is computed by dividing total costs by the number of units produced or by adding average fixed costs (AFC) and average variable costs (AVC). Fixed costs are those costs that remain constant, or do not change, as output varies. Variable costs are those costs that vary in proportion to output.

3. *Marginal cost* (MC) is the increase in the total cost resulting from the production of one more unit of output.

4. *Total revenue* (TR) is the amount of revenue or income received from the sale of a given quantity of goods or services. It is computed by multiplying average revenue, or price, by the number of units sold.

5. *Average revenue* (AR) is the revenue per unit sold, or price. It is computed by dividing the total revenue by the number of units sold.

6. *Marginal revenue* (MR) is the increase in total revenue resulting from the sale of one more unit of output. It is computed by dividing the increase in total revenue resulting from the use of an additional unit of input by the increase in total product.

7. *Total profit* is the difference between total revenue and total cost. Pure profit is the return to the entrepreneur

Exhibit P-3
Characteristics of Various Market Situations

Type of market	Number of Producers	Similarity of Products	Control over Price	Freedom of entry by other firms	Degree of economic profit made by firm (Price – AC × O)	Example
Perfect competition	Many suppliers	Identical	None	Easy	None	Many farm products
Monopoly	One supplier	Product is unique and has no substitutes	Total (except for governmental regulation)	None	Yes	Utilities
Monopolistic competition	Many suppliers but not as many as under pure competition	Similar products with real or perceived differences	Limited but less than monopoly	Only slightly restricted	Yes in short run; tends to be eliminated in long run.	Retail establishments, gasoline stations, some motels
Oligopoly	Few producers	Similar products	Considerable but less than monopoly and more than competition	Highly restricted	Yes	Aluminum, steel, iron, automobile

from the operation of the business, exclusive of any return from the use of the other factors of production.

8. *Short run* is considered the period of time in which some of the factors of production are fixed.

9. *Long run* is considered a period of time in which all factors of production are variable.

Pricing under Perfect Competition. In perfect competition, the price of a commodity is determined by the intersection of the market demand curve and the market supply curve for the commodity or product. Sellers have no pricing problems since their action alone cannot change price. They either sell at the market price or not at all. The firm can sell any amount of the product or service at the price established by the market.

To illustrate the short-run equilibrium of a firm operating under perfect competition, assume the cost and revenue data shown in Exhibit P-4.

Exhibit P-4
Operating Conditions of a Firm Under Perfect Competition

Quantity	Price	Revenue			Costs			Profit*
		Total	Average	Marginal	Total	Average	Marginal	
0	$10	0	0		$6	0		0
				$10			6	
1	10	10	$10		12	12		(2)
				10			4	
2	10	20	10		16	8		(6)
				10			9	
3	10	30	10		25	8⅓		(5)
				10			10	
4	10	40	10		35	8¾		5
				10			12	
5	10	50	10		47	9⅖		3

*Total revenue minus total costs.

The Exhibit offers two approaches to the production problem for the firm operating under perfect competition:

1. Total profit approach: The firm should produce 4 units to maximize profit in the amount of $5 at the point where total revenue ($40) exceeds total cost ($35).

2. Marginal approach: The firm should produce 4 units.

The firm should produce at a level that maximizes profit, i.e., at the point where total revenue exceeds total costs, which is also the point where marginal revenue is positive. Using the total profit approach, the firm should produce four units where total revenue ($40) exceeds total cost ($35). Using the marginal revenue approach, the firm should produce four units where the production of the fourth unit produces marginal revenue of $10 which equals marginal costs of $10.

Under perfect competition, the price a firm receives is identical with average revenue and marginal revenue. When graphed, the average revenue function of the firm is also the demand function for the output of the firm. When graphed, the demand curves are horizontal because a single firm has no effect on price. When the cost and revenue functions are combined, an equilibrium level of output for the firm exists. In long-run equilibrium, marginal cost, average cost, average revenue, and price are equal. Cost and revenue curves for a firm operating under perfect competition are shown in Exhibit P-5.

Exhibit P-5
Costs and Revenue Curves for a Firm Operating Under Perfect Competition

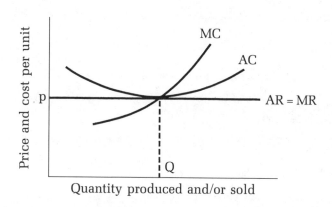

Quantity produced and/or sold

Normal profit refers to the return required to keep productive resources employed. Economic profit is a return above that required to keep productive resources employed. In a competitive market, firms make only a normal profit in the long run. Consumers benefit because the product is sold at the lowest possible price. In perfect competition, market efficiency is present since price equals marginal cost. Output is at its greatest and lowest cost when compared to other market situations.

Monopoly. In a monopoly, the firm has one distinctly downward sloping demand curve. By varying its output, the monopolist can affect the price for its product. Generally, the cost curves for a monopolist do not differ from the cost curves encountered by firms operating under pure competition and other market situations. The demand, or revenue, aspect of monopoly make it distinctive. A monopoly has a marginal revenue curve that differs from its average revenue curve because each time a monopolist sells more output, it must reduce its price. The monopolist seeks to maximize profits. The monopolist increases output as long as marginal revenue from the increased output exceeds the marginal cost of such output. On a graph, this point is at the intersection of the marginal revenue and marginal cost curves. This point determines both output (on the X axis) and price (on the Y axis) at the average revenue curve (see Exhibit P-6, where point *a* equals price; point X equals output).

Profit is the difference between average cost per unit and average revenue per unit. On the graph, the profit area is represented by the shaded rectangular area between the two average curves.

The monopolist has an influence over price because of his ability to control the quantity of goods or services produced. In fact, price is determined by the quantity of output the monopolist is willing to supply, given his demand curves. The monopolist makes an economic profit which is computed as follows:

(Price - Average Cost) x Quantity

Total, average, and marginal revenue for a monopolistic firm are shown in Exhibit P-6. Note that the monopolist sells at a price above its average cost. From the producer's viewpoint, monopolistic conditions are highly desirable. From the consumer's viewpoint, the situation is undesirable because the consumer must pay a higher price for goods or services produced under monopoly than under perfect competition. Industries which operate under conditions of decreasing cost tend to promote the existence of monopolies since one large supplier can eliminate smaller competitors because of production cost advantages associated with economies of scale.

Monopolistic Competition. Under conditions of monopolistic competition, a firm is able to differentiate its product from similar products. The producer has a downward-sloping demand curve (average revenue curve) which indicates that as prices decline, demand increases. In the short run, firms operating under conditions of monopolistic competition have

---

Exhibit P-6
Cost and Revenue Curves of a Monopolist

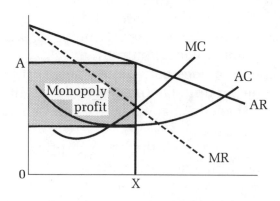

---

an equilibrium position similar to the monopolistic firm, i.e., at the point where MR = MC from below and where price is equal to or larger than average variable cost. The firm makes an economic profit but not as large a profit as a firm would make operating under monopolistic conditions (see Exhibit P-7).

Exhibit P–7
Monopolistic Competition

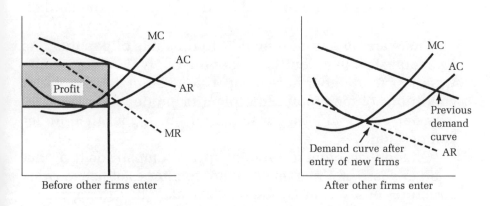

Before other firms enter   After other firms enter

Firms operating under conditions of monopolistic competition usually have excess capacity because they are not operating at a level of output where average cost is lowest. In the long run, new firms enter the market because of the presence of economic profit. Firms do not operate at the optimum of their cost curves and so have not attained their greatest efficiency.

Oligopoly. Under oligopolistic market conditions, firms in the arrangement are interdependent and recognize this fact. Any action taken by one member will usually result in a reaction by the other firms, which are rivals.

If the firms agree to maximize the joint profits of all the firms in the market, each firm may maximize its own profits. On the other hand, a firm may attempt to pursue policies designed to maximize its individual profits, ignoring the reaction of its rivals. The behavior of the rivals will determine the success or failure of this effort. Joint maximization of profit is usually achieved when:

1. the firms recognize their interdependencies;

2. the ease with which the firms can agree on output and price, which usually requires collusion or cartels, and

3. the ease with which other firms can enter the market.

There are no standard models to illustrate oligopolies. As a general statement, output under oligopoly would be somewhat less than under pure competition and more than under conditions of monopoly. Idle plant or productivity capacity exists and prices to the consumer will be higher than under competition.

Oligopolists often resort to nonprice competition to attract a larger share of a market so as not to alter established price structures or invite price wars with rivals. They attempt to do this through advertising, product differentiation, product innovation, and other means.

Oligopolists often form cartels to establish price and output among the member firms. Policies are sometimes determined by a price or production leader. In some situations, a firm not necessarily the dominant member is recognized as the firm which assumes a leadership role. These procedures suggest that oligopolists use a form of administered price structure.

Pricing Decisions. The economic model of pricing that relies on marginal cost and marginal revenue has many problems when applied in practice. Companies frequently are unable to obtain adequate information about the price-quantity relationships of their products. Small errors in this area can produce sizeable errors in marginal revenue. Factors other than price often determine the quantity sold, including the advertising and promotion a product is given, distribution channels used, the credit policy of the firm, and others.

Research indicates important factors affecting pricing decisions include company goals (e.g., target return, profit maximization, market share), costs, consumer demand, competition, legal influences, and social responsibilities.

This entry in the encyclopedia described the economic theory underlying the pricing decisions. Other entries in the encyclopedia describe alternatives to the economic model and can be located under the general heading "Pricing Policy."

See also Free enterprise system; Pricing policy.

REFERENCE
Fallon, William K., ed., *AMA Management Handbook* (AMACOM, New York, 1983).

PRICING POLICY: "FAIR" PRICING

"Fair" pricing is an ethical concept of pricing goods and services. Under fair pricing, an organization should price its goods and services at a price that allows the full recovery of all costs plus an equitable profit. Costs incurred for factors of production (land, labor, and capital) are supposed to be in amounts that provide for a fair standard of living for the parties involved. "Fair" pricing is difficult to apply in that the concept of "fair" or "equitable" is difficult to define.

See also Pricing policy.

PRICING POLICY: GAME THEORY

Some firms apply game theory to develop pricing policies. A game is a competitive situation where two or more persons pursue their own interests and no person can dictate the outcome of the game. The game's outcome depends upon each player's strategies. Game theory is related to operations research and decision theory. Key concepts associated with game theory include:

1. *Game*—a situation involving a conflict.
2. *Strategy*—a plan or objective that is selected before action begins.
3. *Payoff*—the value of the game to a player.
4. *Zero-sum game*—a game in which all payoffs for all players total zero; what one player gains the other loses.
5. *Non-zero-sum game*—a game in which all the payoffs for all players do not total zero.

To illustrate game theory with a simple example, assume that a firm has three strategies available against a competitor who has four courses of action. A payoff matrix is constructed which shows the percentage-points increases or decreases in market share to the manager of the firm:

| | | Competitor's strategies | | | |
		No. 1	No. 2	No. 3	No. 4
Our firm's	No. 1	.50	.10	– 1.3	.20
strategies	No. 2	.90	.15	.25	.30
	No. 3	.02	.0	– .04	– .06

If our firm selects its first strategy and the competitor selects his fourth strategy, our firm will increase its share of the market by .20 percent. According to one application of game theory, the firm should first select the minimum payoffs for each strategy:

Strategy	Minimum Payoff
No. 1	– 1.3
No. 2	0.15
No. 3	– 0.6

The firm would then choose strategy No. 2 and gain 15 percentage points of the market. By choosing this strategy, the firm will maximize its minimum possible gain, regardless of countermoves by a competitor.

The competitor would select the worst that can happen to him under each of his four strategies. From this list, he selects the least unfavorable event. By such action, he minimizes his maximum loss:

Competitor strategy	Maximum Loss
No. 1	.90
No. 2	.15
No. 3	.25
No. 4	.30

The competitor chooses action No. 2 in which case it loses 15 percentage points of the market. In our case, the payoff value for the firm equals the payoff value for the competitor, i.e., 15 percentage points. When the two values differ, the players would use mixed strategies where the specific strategy to be used is selected randomly with a determined probability.

See also Pricing policy; Quantitative methods; Negotiating process.

REFERENCE
Bierman, Harold, Jr., Bonini, Charles P., Fouraker, Lawrence E., Jaedicke, Robert K., *Quantitative Analysis for Business Decisions* (Irwin, Homewood, IL, latest edition).

PRICING POLICY: PENETRATION PRICING
Companies have occasionally used penetration pricing in order to gain entrance into a market. In penetration pricing, the company introduces a product at a low price and then hopefully moves up to a higher price. Penetration pricing is sometimes used when the competition dictates a price ceiling. Where a

high volume of sales is required to make a product profitable, penetration pricing with its low prices might produce the necessary volume.

See also Pricing policy.

PRICING POLICY: REGULATED PRICES

Prices of some goods and services are established by government regulatory bodies. Public utilities (natural gas, water, electricity, and telephone) are a prime example. Prices are usually established by regulatory commissions on a full-cost-plus basis. Once the price is set, the commission periodically reviews the price structure to allow the utility to recover full cost plus a return on the owners' investment. Government pricing regulation is usually for the purpose of preventing excessive profits, to provide a subsidy for the perceived desirable industries (air service), or to discourage consumption (alcohol).

See also Pricing policy; Free enterprise system; Government regulation.

PRICING POLICY: RETURN ON ASSETS

Some firms establish a price for their product or service based on a desired rate of return on assets employed in the company. The desired markup on cost can be determined according to the following formula and illustration; the company desires a 10 percent return on $60,000,000 assets employed in the business and annual costs total $45,000,000:

$$\text{Percent markup on cost} = \frac{\text{Assets employed}}{\text{Total annual costs}} \times \frac{\text{Desired rate of return}}{\text{capital employed}}$$

$$\text{Percent markup on cost} = \frac{\$60,000,000}{\$45,000,000} \times 10\%$$

$$\text{Percent markup} = 13.3\%$$

The sales volume would then be computed using this formula:

Sales volume = Total annual + (Total annual × Percentage markup
                  costs   costs   on cost)

Sales volume = $45,000,000 + ($45,000,000 × 13.3 percent)

Sales volume = $50,985,000 (rounded to $51,000,000)

If one million units are expected to be sold, the sales price should be $51.00 ($51,000,000/1,000,000 units).

Sales volume could also be computed directly by multiplying the capital employed by desired rate of return on assets and added to the total annual costs:

[($60,000 × 10%)] + $45,000,000 = $51,000,000

The return on investment model assumes that the company will be able to make sales at the price determined and in the quantities assumed. Competition may force the price lower; the absence of competition may enable the firm to adjust the price upward.

See also Pricing policy; Return on investment.

PRICING POLICY: SKIM-OFF-THE-TOP PRICING

If a company's product or service is unique or novel, the company may be able to take advantage of this situation until the market demand declines or competitors enter the field. Pricing under such conditions is referred to as skim-off-the-top pricing, or price skimming. As long as the company maintained an exclusive market for this product, the company could charge a higher than normal price for the product in the early marketing stages. Generally, a higher price will produce a larger dollar volume of sales initially than would a low initial price.

See also Pricing policy.

PRICING POLICY: STANDARD COSTS

Standard costs are costs that could be attained with efficient production methods at a normal capacity. In standard cost systems, a standard cost for material, labor, and factory overhead is developed. When a standard costs pricing policy is adopted, the company adds a desired markup to standard costs to establish a price.

See also Pricing policy.

PRICING POLICY: STAY-OUT, FLOOR, AND GOING-RATE PRICING

Stay-out pricing refers to low initial pricing which is directed at discouraging potential competitors from entering the market. When stay-out pricing is used, profit margins are low and competitors may find it difficult to compete under such circumstances.

Floor pricing involves lowering prices to meet competitors' prices. A floor pricing policy frequently results in little or no profit but is justified on the basis that such pricing is required for the firm to keep its product(s) in the market.

Many firms simply adopt a manufacturer's or wholesalers's suggested retail price as a convenience or because contracts require it. Going-rate pricing requires a seller to base his prices on prices established by competitors in his market.

See also Pricing policy.

PRICING POLICY: STRATEGIES

Pricing policy and pricing strategies are affected by such factors as organizational objectives, cost, competition, and demand. Pricing strategies must take these factors into consideration. Pricing strategies for a variety of situations and conditions will be discussed.

1. Pricing strategies for new product.

   a. Skimming pricing. Skimming pricing sets a relatively high price during the initial stage of a product's life cycle. When the uniqueness of the product has lessened, the company has the opportunity to lower its price and market the product on the mass market.

   b. Penetration pricing. When penetration pricing is used, a company sets a relatively low price during the initial stages of a product's life to discourage competition so that a large market share can be obtained.

2. Pricing strategies for established products.

   a. Maintain the price to maintain the company's market position and profitability.

   b. Reduce the price to meet the competition (a defensive action), to beat the competition, or to respond to demand.

   c. Increase the price to take advantage of product differential, to maintain profit targets during inflation, or to segment the market.

3. Price-flexibility strategy.

   a. One-price strategy to retain steady profit margins, to simplify pricing and marketing decisions, to retain customer goodwill, or to avoid government regulation.

   b. Flexible-pricing strategy to increase sales, to maximize short-term profits, to increase market share, and to position the firm to adjust to competition.

4. Product-line-pricing strategy. Product-line-pricing strategy requires that a product line is priced according to each product's impact on and relationships with other products in the line. The objective of this strategy is to maximize profit.

5. Bundling-pricing strategy. Bundling-pricing strategy provides a margin in the price sufficient to cover support and service functions required to market the product. Bundling-pricing is frequently used in leasing arrangements.

6. Price-leadership strategy is adopted by the leading firm, not necessarily the largest, in the industry in making price moves, which are subsequently followed by other firms in the industry. Price-leadership encourages stability in price movements, lessens the potential for price wars, and contributes to a maintenance of market share within the industry.

7. Pricing strategy to build market share. Building market share typically requires setting the lowest price for new products, or reducing the price for existing products. This strategy frequently results in establishing barriers to entry to the industry by competitors and frequently to cost leadership.

PRICING POLICY: TRANSFER PRICING

Divisions of an enterprise frequently buy and sell to one another. A price must be established for these transfers. This price is referred to as the transfer price. Various alternatives to establishing a transfer price include the following:

1. The transfer price should be set equal to the manufacturing cost of the selling division.

2. The transfer price should be the amount the selling division could sell the product to an outside firm.

3. The transfer price should be the amount the buying division could purchase the product from an outside firm.

4. The transfer price should be a negotiated amount agreed upon by the buying and selling divisions.

5. The transfer price should be the costs incurred to the point of transfer plus the opportunity costs for the firm as a whole. The opportunity cost would be the next best alternative for the firm. For example, if the selling division was operating at less than full capacity, the opportunity cost would be zero. If the selling division was operating at full capacity, the opportunity cost would be the lost contribution margin (selling price minus variable costs) resulting from forgoing outside sales to sell to the buying division.

The choice of method depends upon a number of factors, such as the autonomy allowed to divisions, the degree of market competition, the extent to which the goals of the division are expected to correspond to the goals of the firm, short-run supply and demand relationships, and how divisions are evaluated by the firm.

See also Pricing policy.

PRICING POLICY: VARIABLE COST PRICING

Variable cost pricing requires that a firm identify its variable and fixed costs. When this distinction can be made, a company's contribution margin (sales minus variable costs) can be computed. The effect on contribution margins of different prices can be related to fixed costs. Assume that a company produces two products and the variable cost of material, labor, and factory overhead for Product X is $20 and for Product Y is $30. If a 25 percent markup on variable cost is used, the sales price is

	Product X	Product Y
Full cost (assumed)	$50	$40
Markup on variable cost:		
10% × $20	2	
10% × $30		3
Sales price	$52	$43

P

A major advantage of variable cost pricing is that the difficult problem of allocating indirect, fixed costs can be avoided. Variable pricing is often useful in pricing a special order at a special price, in a dumping situation, or in a distress case. In difficult times, a company may need to make some revenue above variable cost as an alternative to no revenue. Special-order pricing may involve discriminatory prices which may have to be justified in order not to violate the Robinson-Patman Act.

See also Pricing policy; Cost behavior; Direct costing and absorption costing.

Q

QUALITATIVE CHARACTERISTICS OF ACCOUNTING INFORMATION

Qualitative characteristics of accounting information are those qualities or ingredients of accounting information that make it useful. The FASB's Statement of Financial Accounting Concepts No. 2, *Qualitative Characteristics of Accounting Information*, discusses the qualitative characteristics that make accounting information useful and are the qualities to be sought when accounting choices are made. The diagram in Exhibit Q-1 outlines what is referred to as a hierarchy of accounting information qualities. Exhibit Q-2 provides a summary of definitions used in Exhibit Q-1.

The hierarchical arrangement is used to show certain relationships among the qualities. The hierarchy shows that information useful for decision making is the most important. The primary qualities are that accounting information shall be relevant and reliable. If either of these two qualities is completely missing, the information cannot be useful. To be relevant, information must be timely, and it must have predictive value or feedback value or both. To be reliable, information must have representational faithfulness and it must be verifiable and neutral. Comparability, including consistency, is a secondary quality that interacts with relevance and reliability

281

Exhibit Q–1

Qualitative Characteristics of Accounting Information

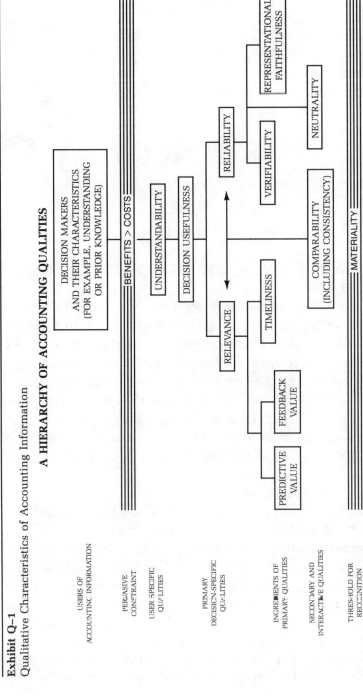

A HIERARCHY OF ACCOUNTING QUALITIES

USERS OF
ACCOUNTING INFORMATION

PERVASIVE
CONSTRAINT

USER SPECIFIC
QUALITIES

PRIMARY
DECISION-SPECIFIC
QUALITIES

INGREDIENTS OF
PRIMARY QUALITIES

SECONDARY AND
INTERACTIVE QUALITIES

THRESHOLD FOR
RECOGNITION

DECISION MAKERS
AND THEIR CHARACTERISTICS
(FOR EXAMPLE, UNDERSTANDING
OR PRIOR KNOWLEDGE)

BENEFITS > COSTS

UNDERSTANDABILITY

DECISION USEFULNESS

RELEVANCE

RELIABILITY

TIMELINESS

PREDICTIVE
VALUE

FEEDBACK
VALUE

VERIFIABILITY

REPRESENTATIONAL
FAITHFULNESS

NEUTRALITY

COMPARABILITY
(INCLUDING CONSISTENCY)

MATERIALITY

Source: Statement of Financial Accounting Concepts No. 2, "Qualitative Characteristics of Accounting Information" (Stamford, FASB, May 1980). Copyright by Financial Accounting Standards Board, High Ridge Park, Stamford, Connecticut 06905, U.S.A. Reprinted with permission.

Exhibit Q-2

Qualitative Characteristics of Accounting Information

Bias Bias in measurement is the tendency of a measure to fall more often on one side than the other of what it represents instead of being equally likely to fall on either side. Bias in accounting measures means a tendency to be consistently too high or too low.

Comparability The quality of information that enables users to identify similarities in and differences between two sets of economic phenomena.

Completeness The inclusion in reported information of everything material that is necessary for faithful representation of the relevant phenomena.

Conservatism A prudent reaction to uncertainty to try to insure that uncertainty and risks inherent in business situations are adequately considered.

Consistency Conformity from period to period with unchanging policies and procedures.

Feedback Value The quality of information that enables users to confirm or correct prior expectations.

Materiality The magnitude of an omission or misstatement of accounting information that, in the light of surrounding circumstances, makes it probable that the judgment of a resonable person relying on the information would have been changed or influenced by the omission or misstatement.

Neutrality Absence in reported information of bias intended to attain a predetermined result or to induce a particular mode of behavior.

Predictive Value The quality of information that helps users to increase the likelihood of correctly forecasting the outcome of past or present events.

Relevance The capacity of information to make a difference in a decision by helping users to form predictions about the outcomes of past, present, and future events or to confirm or correct prior expectations.

Reliability The quality of information that assures that information is reasonably free from error and bias and faithfully represents what it purports to represent.

Representational Faithfulness Correspondence or agreement between a measure or description and the phenomenon that it purports to represent (sometimes called validity).

Timeliness Having information available to a decision maker before it loses its capacity to influence decisions.

Understandability The quality of information that enables users to perceive its significance.

Verifiability The ability through consensus among measures to ensure that information represents what it purports to represent or that the chosen method of measurement has been used without error or bias.

Source: FASB, *Accounting Standards: Statement of Financial Accounting Concepts 1-6*, McGraw-Hill Book Company, New York, 1986.

and contributes to the overall usefulness of information. Two constraints are shown on the chart: benefits must exceed costs, and materiality. To be useful and worth providing, the benefits of information should exceed its cost. All of the qualities described are subject to a materiality threshold. Materiality refers to whether the magnitude of an omission or misstatement of accounting information would influence the judgment of a reasonable person relying on the information.

Information provided by financial reporting should be understandable to those who have a reasonable understanding of business and economic activities and are willing to study the information with reasonable diligence.

The hierarchy of qualitative characteristics does not rank the characteristics. If information is to be useful, all characteristics are required to a minimum degree. At times various qualities may conflict in particular circumstances, in which event trade-offs are often necessary or appropriate. For example, the most relevant information may be difficult to understand, or information that is easy to understand may not be very relevant.

See also Accounting; Information; Information systems.

REFERENCE
SFAC No. 2, *Qualitative Characteristics of Accounting Information* (Financial Accounting Standards Board, Stamford, Conn.).

QUALITY CIRCLES
The major improvements in production and quality of Japanese industry has been attributed, in part, to quality circles (Q.C.s). Quality circles are small groups of workers who meet periodically to consider work-related problems and opportunities, including quality of work, quantity of work, costs, evaluations, and other matters. Companies which exploit quality circles are characterized by the following features:

1. human resource management: job security and job opportunity; strong personal commitment to organizational goals and objectives,

2. group dynamics in problem solving and participation in management,

3. world market penetration and manipulation, and

4. ability to adapt management to a national culture.

Quality circles, as a management technique, are said to have certain advantages:

1. They serve to satisfy needs of employees to participate in planning and improving their work.

2. They provide challenges and growth opportunities for the employees.

3. They serve as positive motivators for the work force.

U.S. companies have experienced certain problems associated with using quality circles:

1. worker resistance,

2. union resistence, and

3. supervisor resistance.

It has been found that to implement Q.C.s as an organizing arrangement,

1. management should prepare the organizational environment before introducing the procedure,

2. management should have a long-term commitment to the project,

3. top management support and involvement should be visible and consistent,

4. the authority and responsibilities of the quality circles should be clearly established,

5. participants should be thoroughly trained in the process and techniques associated with Q.C.s, and

6. recommendations coming from Q.C.s should be given serious consideration by management.

See also Control function; Performance evaluation; Quality control.

REFERENCE
Ingle, Sud, *Quality Circles Master Guide* (Prentice-Hall, Englewood Cliffs, NJ, 1982).

QUALITY CONTROL

Quality is considered one of the components of efficiency, the others being speed, resource utilization, service, and changeability. Quality control refers to adherence to standards or requirements for goods and services produced or received. Quality control provides a degree of assurance to product/service performance. Total quality performance has been defined by A. V. Feigenbaum as "an effective system for integrating the quality development, quality maintenance and quality improvement efforts of the various groups in an organization so as to enable production and service at the most economical level which allow for full customer satisfaction." Inspection and observation are the major activities by which qualitative or quantitative quality controls are monitored. Quality control has its costs:

1. cost of conformance: costs associated with preventing defects, e.g., product design review, vendor approval, process controls, inspection, testing, etc., and

2. cost of nonconformance: costs associated with product/ service defects or failure, e.g., rework or redesign, returns and allowances, product liability, etc.

Quality can be improved if management includes quality in both its short- and long-range planning activities and is committed to a policy of quality control. Quality control is essentially management's responsibility. Personnel motivation can be a strong and effective factor in developing product and service quality. "Zero defect" programs in production processes can be an effective quality control technique if top management is committed and involved.

See also Efficiency and effectiveness; Planning function; Control function; Quality circles.

REFERENCE
Feigenbaum, A.V., *Total Quality Control* (McGraw-Hill, New York, 1983).

QUANTITATIVE METHODS
Become of the complexity of management, managers have turned to quantitative techniques and models as tools for solving many problems. Such methods are frequently referred to as Operations Research (OR).

A rational approach to quantitative decision making involves establishing a well-defined objective, selecting a mathematical or logical model, and arranging an optimization process. Quantitative methods include models that:

1. establish equations that can be solved mathematically, and

2. simulation models.

Q

Linear programming will be used to demonstrate quantitative method techniques. Other quantitative methods are illustrated throughout this encyclopedia. Linear programming is a powerful mathematical procedure designed to assist in planning activities. Most linear programming problems call for the maximization or minimization of some economic objective such as net income, net loss, or costs. These problems often involve the determination of the optimum scheduling routine, product mix, production routing, or transportation route. In such problems, constraints usually exist on available alternatives—for example, constraints on available resources, machine time, manpower, or facilities.

Linear programming problems can be solved by a variety of mathematical approaches, such as the simplex method. Linear programming computer programs are available.

To illustrate linear programming, a linear programming model for a product-mix problem will be presented. Assume that a firm has two machines that are used in the production of Products A and B. Machine X has 24 hours of excess capacity. Machine Y has 16 hours of excess capacity. Production of one unit of Product A requires 4 machine hours on each machine; Product B requires 6 machine hours per unit on Machine X and 2 machine hours per unit on Machine Y. Product A has a contribution margin of $5. Product B has a contribution margin of $65. The firm wants to know whether to use the excess capacity of the machines to produce Product A or Product B or a mix of the two. The firm wants to maximize net income.

This problem can be solved through the following steps.

1. *State the objective.* Set up an equation that expresses the quantity to be maximized (or minimized) in terms of the factors that can be varied as part of the decision to be made. In this case, the equation should express the contribution to net income as a function of the number of units of each product to be produced. This equation is referred to as the profit function. Let X-a be

288

the number of units of Product A to be produced, X-b, the number of units of Product B to be produced, and P, the total contribution margin for the production using the excess machine capacity. The output function is:

$$P = (X\text{-}a \times \$5) + (X\text{-}b \times \$6)$$

The problem is to find the values of X-a and X-b that will maximize P.

2. *Identify limiting factors.* Establish equations that express the constraints imposed upon the solution. In this case, the constraints are (1) that 24 hours of machine time are available on Machine X and 16 hours on Machine Y; (2) that it takes 4 hours to produce a unit of Product B on Machine X, and 2 hours to produce a unit of Product B on Machine Y; and (3) that no negative production is possible. These constraints can be expressed by the following four inequalities:

$$(X\text{-}a \times 4 \text{ hours}) + (X\text{-}b \times 6 \text{ hours}) \leqslant 24 \text{ hours};$$
$$(X\text{-}a \times 4 \text{ hours}) + (X\text{-}b \times 2 \text{ hours}) \leqslant 16 \text{ hours};$$
$$X\text{-}a \geqslant O$$
$$X\text{-}b \geqslant O$$

3. *To solve the problem graphically, plot the constraint inequalities on a graph (see Exhibit Q-3).* In this case, the third and fourth inequalities limit possible solutions to the area in the uper right quadrant of the graph. The first and second inequalities complete the boundaries of the shaded polygon. This polygon is the area of possible solutions that lie within the constraints imposed by the problem.

Q

Graphic Identification of Possible Solutions to Linear Programming Problem

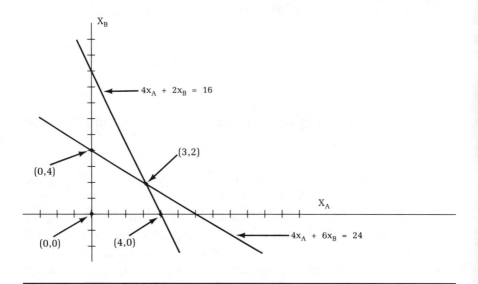

4. *Identify possible solutions.* Of the various parts of values for X-a and X-b that lie within the area of possible solutions, which pair of values gives the maximum value for P (see step 1)? The optimum solution will always be one of the corner points of the polygon. A list of all the corner points and the value of P computed for each point is shown here:

Corner points	(X-a × $5)	+	(X-b × $6)	=	P(Profit)
(0,0)	(0 × $5)	+	(0 × $6)	=	$ 0
(4,0)	(4 × $5)	+	(0 × $6)	=	20
(0,4)	(0 × $5)	+	(4 × $6)	=	24
(3,2)	(3 × $5)	+	(2 × $6)	=	27

Moving from one corner point to another represents a substitution of units of one product for units of the other. The corner point (3,2) gives the maximum value of P. That is, the maximum profit (contribution to net income) can be obtained by using the excess machine capacity to produce 3 units of Product A and 2 units of Product B.

See also Planning function; Control function; Pricing policy; Management.

REFERENCE
Bierman, Harold, Jr., Bonini, Charles P., Fouraker, Lawrence E., and Jaedicke, Robert K., *Quantitative Analysis for Business Decisions* (Irwin, Homewood, IL., latest edition).

R

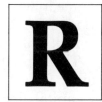

RATIOS

A ratio is an expression of a mathematical relationship between one quantity and another. The ratio of 400 to 200 is 2:1 or 2. If a ratio is to have any utility, the elements which constitute the ratio must express a meaningful relationship. For example, there is a relationship between accounts receivable and sales, between net income and total assets, and between current assets and current liabilities. Ratio analysis can disclose relationships which reveal conditions and trends that often cannot be noted by inspection of the individual components of the ratio.

Ratios are generally not significant of themselves but assume significance when they are compared with previous ratios of the same firm, ratios of other enterprises in the same industry, and ratios of the industry within which the company operates.

It is helpful to organize ratios in terms of areas to be analyzed and interpreted. At least three major areas can be identified:

1. Short-term liquidity.

2. Capital structure (and long-term solvency).

3. Earnings and profitability.

Short-term liquidity refers to the ability of a firm to meet its current obligations as they mature. The relationship of current assets to current liabilities is an important indicator of the degree to which a firm is liquid. Working capital and the components of working capital also provide measures of the liquidity of a firm.

The capital structure of an enterprise consists of debt and equity funds. The sources and composition of the two types of capital determine to a considerable extent the financial stability and long-term solvency of the firm. A company's capitalization usually depends on the industry, the financial position of the company, and the philosophy of management. Long-term debt and preferred stock can add "leverage" to a company's capital structure. Capital structure ratios provide information on the debt capacity of the company and its level of financial risk. Financing decisions frequently involve determining the type of arrangements to be used and the amount of indebtedness to be incurred. Debt typically has the following advantages and disadvantages:

1. Advantages:

   a. Interest is a known cost.

   b. Debt usually confers no unpredictable claim on future earnings.

   c. Interest is tax deductible.

   d. Debt generally does not involve a dilution of owners' equity.

   e. Debt offers the potential for positive financial leverage to operate (but negative leverage is also a possibility).

2. Disadvantages:

   a. Interest is a fixed cost which must be paid in difficult times.

b. Interest is a fixed cost which increases the break-even point for the company.

c. Payments for interest and the retirement of the debt involve cash outflows.

d. Outstanding debt typically restricts additional financing opportunities and can include restrictive covenants.

The advantages and disadvantages claimed for equity financing include:

1. Advantages:

a. Equity does not involve a fixed cost.

b. Equity typically requires no defined payback.

c. Equity issuances typically do not place major restrictions on management.

2. Disadvantages:

a. Dilution of earnings and ownership is possible.

b. Equity provides the new investor with a degree of control over the affairs of the business.

Operating and profitability performance ratios reflect the results of the profit-seeking activities of an enterprise. Much of the data required for evaluating performance is obtained directly from the income statement which summarizes the results of operations. However, performance should be related to the assets which produce the earnings and how outsiders (e.g., the stock market) perceive the performance and earnings of the enterprise. Measures of operating performance usually provide answers to the following questions: How much profit does the company make on each dollar of investment? How much profit does the company make on each dollar of sales? The profitability of investment usually relates to the following:

1. Return on total assets (total investment).
2. Return on invested capital (debt and equity).
3. Return on owners' investment (shareholders' equity).

The profitability of sales focuses on specific contributions of purchasing, production, administration and overall profitability as reflected in gross profit margin, operating profit margin, and net profit margin.

Several important profitability ratios are referred to as "market value" ratios. Most of these ratios relate to the valuation of stock and are of considerable importance to financial analysts and stockholders. These ratios include earnings per share, dividend per share, yield on common stock, dividend payout, and book value per share of common stock. Major financial ratios are illustrated in Exhibit R-3. Data for the problem illustrated is provided in Exhibits R-1 and R-2.

See also Financial statement analysis; Leverage; Return-on-investment analysis; Liquidity; Working capital; Forecasting financial requirements.

REFERENCES
Bernstein, Leopold A., *Financial Statement Analysis* (Richard D. Irwin, Homewood, IL, 1983).
Coleman, Almand, et al, *Financial Accounting and Statement Analysis: A Manager's Guide* (Robert F. Dame, Richmond, VA, 1982).

RESPONSIBILITY ACCOUNTING
Responsibility accounting focuses on the collection of data to place responsibility for cost incurrence on managers to achieve cost control. The emphasis is on people—who incurred the costs. Responsibility accounting is also referred to as profit-

Exhibit R–1
Balance Sheet Used in Exhibit R.3

R. N. Services Company
Balance sheet
December 31, 19X0 and 19X1

	19X1	19X0
Assets		
Current assets:		
Cash	$ 50,000	$ 35,000
Marketable securities	100,000	65,000
Accounts receivable	200,000	250,000
Inventories	80,000	60,000
Total current assets	430,000	400,000
Property, plant, and equipment	1,000,000	800,000
Less accumulated depreciation	(600,000)	(500,000)
	400,000	300,000
Goodwill	100,000	125,000
Total assets	$1,330,000	$825,000
Liabilities and shareholders' equity		
Current liabilities		
Accounts payable	$ 100,000	$100,000
Notes payable	15,000	15,000
Income taxes payable	100,000	85,000
Total current liabilites	215,000	200,000
Long-term debt:		
Bonds and notes payable	500,000	350,000
Total liabilities	715,000	550,000
Stockholders' equity:		
Common stock, 10,000 shares outstanding	250,000	200,000
Contributed capital in excess of par	100,000	100,000
Retained earnings	265,000	25,000
Total equity	615,000	325,000
Total liabilities and shareholders' equity	$1,330,000	$825,000

Exhibit R–2
Income Statement Used in Exhibit R.3

R. N. Services Company
Income statement
For the years ended December 31, 19X0 and 19X1

	19X1	19X0
Net sales	$625,000	$225,000
Costs and expenses		
Cost of goods sold	100,000	70,000
Selling and administrative expense	150,000	100,000
Interest expense	50,000	30,000
Total costs and expenses	300,000	200,000
Income before income taxes	325,000	25,000
Income taxes	75,000	5,000
Net income	250,000	20,000
Retained earnings at beginning of period	25,000	5,000
Dividends	10,000	0
Retained earnings at end of period	$265,000	$ 25,000

Additional information:
Market price per share of common stock, $75.
Average daily purchases of inventory, $50,000.

Exhibit R-3
Liquidity, Solvency, and Profitability Ratios

Ratio	Formula	Solution to case	Interpretation
Liquidity ratios			
a. Current (or working capital) ratio	$\dfrac{\text{Current assets}}{\text{Current liabilities}}$	$\dfrac{\$430,000}{\$215,000} = 2$	Short-term debt-paying ability (i.e., dollar amount of current assets from which to obtain funds necessary to liquidate each dollar of current liabilities).
b. Acid-test (or quick) ratio	$\dfrac{\text{Quick assets, i.e., cash marketable securities, receivables}}{\text{Current liabilities}}$	$\dfrac{\$350,000}{\$215,000} = 1.6$	A more severe test of the short-term debt-paying ability than the current ratio since it excludes inventory (which awaits sale) and prepaid expenses.
c. Cash ratio	$\dfrac{\text{Cash}}{\text{Current liabilities}}$	$\dfrac{\$50,000}{\$215,000} = .23$	The severest test of short-term debt-paying ability.
Measures of the movement or turnover of current assets and liabilities			
a. Receivables turnover	$\dfrac{\text{Sales (net)}}{\text{Average receivables (net)}}$	$\dfrac{\$625,000}{\$225,000} = 2.7$	The efficiency in collecting receivables and in managing credit.
b. Age of receivables	$\dfrac{365}{\text{Receivables turnover}}$	$\dfrac{365}{2.7} = 135$	The number of days it takes on the average to collect accounts receivable; the extent of control over credit and collection.
c. Inventory turnover	$\dfrac{\text{Cost of goods sold}}{\text{Average inventory}}$	$\dfrac{\$100,000}{\$70,000} = 1.4$	Marketability of inventory, efficiency in the management of inventory, and the reasonableness of the quantity of inventory on hand.
d. Days in inventory	$\dfrac{365}{\text{Inventory turnover}}$	$\dfrac{365}{1.4} = 261$	The average number of days required to use or sell inventory (e.g., the average period that an item is held in inventory). For a manufacturing company, the number of days should correspond closely with production time.
e. Working capital turnover	$\dfrac{\text{Net sales}}{\text{Average working capital}}$	$\dfrac{\$625,000}{\$207,500} = 3$	The extent to which a company is using working capital to generate sales.
f. Number of days' purchases in ending accounts payable	$\dfrac{\text{Accounts payable}}{\text{Average daily purchases}}$	$\dfrac{\$100,000}{\$50,000} = 2$	The extent to which the company is paying its bills promptly.
Solvency ratios			
1. Measures of capital structure:			
a. Owners' equity to total assets	$\dfrac{\text{Total owners' equity}}{\text{Total assets (net)}}$	$\dfrac{\$615,000}{\$1,330,000} = .46$	Proportion of firm's assets provided by owner.

Exhibit R-3
Liquidity, Solvency, and Profitability Ratios (Continued)

Ratio	Formula	Solution to case	Interpretation
b. Owners' equity to total liabilities	$\dfrac{\text{Total owner's equity}}{\text{Total liabilities}}$	$\dfrac{\$615,000}{\$715,000} = .86$	Relative claims of owners and creditors to rest of firm.
c. Fixed assets to total equity	$\dfrac{\text{Total owners' equity}}{\text{Fixed assets (net)}}$	$\dfrac{\$615,000}{\$400,000} = 1.53$	Relationship of owners' investment to the company investment in fixed assets (i.e., the higher the ratio, the less owners' capital is available for working capital).
d. Book value per share of common stock	$\dfrac{\text{Common stock equity}}{\text{Number of common shares outstanding}}$	$\dfrac{\$615,000}{10,000} = \$61.50$	Net assets reported on financial statement per share of common stock.
2. Measures of debt structure (debt management):			
a. Total liabilities to total assets	$\dfrac{\text{Total liabilities}}{\text{Total assets (net)}}$	$\dfrac{\$715,000}{\$1,330,000} = .53$	Protection available to creditors and the extent to which the company is trading on equity.
b. Total liabilities to owners' equity	$\dfrac{\text{Total liabilities}}{\text{Owners' equity}}$	$\dfrac{\$715,000}{\$615,000} = 1.2$	Relationship between total debt and equity financing. "What is owed to what is owned."
Profitability (earnings) ratios			
1. Net income to sales	$\dfrac{\text{Net income}}{\text{Net sales}}$	$\dfrac{\$250,000}{\$625,000} = .4$	Profit margin per dollar of sales.
2. Operating ratio	$\dfrac{\text{Cost of goods sold + operating expenses}}{\text{Net sales}}$	$\dfrac{\$100,000 + \$150,000}{\$625,000} = .4$	Profit margin per dollar of sales.
3. Sales to total assets (or asset turnover)	$\dfrac{\text{Net sales}}{\text{Average total assets}}$	$\dfrac{\$625,000}{\$1,077,000} = .57$	Productivity of all assets in generating sales.
4. Earnings per share of common stock	$\dfrac{\text{Net income-preferred dividend requirements}}{\text{Average number of common stock}}$	$\dfrac{\$250,000}{10,000} = \$25$	Return on common shareholders' investment per share of common stock

Exhibit R-3
Liquidity, Solvency, and Profitability Ratios (Continued)

Ratio	Formula	Solution to case	Interpretation
5. Price/earnings ratio	Market price per share of common stock / Net income per share of common stock	$\dfrac{\$75}{\$25} = \$3$	Price paid for stock per dollar of earnings (i.e., the price of earnings). Newspaper include this information in daily stock tables.
6. Dividends yield	Annual cash dividends per share of common stock / Market price per share of common stock	$\dfrac{\$1}{\$75} = .013$	Cash yield or return on common stock.
7. Return on investment (or return on assets	Net income / Average total assets	$\dfrac{\$250,000}{\$1,077,000} = .23$	Return on investment in total assets. Sometimes net operating income is used as the numerator while intangibles and investments are excluded from the denominator.
8. Return on common stockholders' equity	Net income / Average common stockholders' equity	$\dfrac{\$250,000}{\$470,000} = .53$	Return on the investment by common stockholders.
9. Payout ratio	Cash dividends / Net income	$\dfrac{\$10,000}{\$250,000} = .04$	The extent to which a company distributes current earnings to stockholders in the form of dividends i.e., the "generosity" of the Board of Directors.
10. Cash flow from operations per share of common stock	Net income adjusted for noncash items / Average number of shares of common stock outstanding	$\dfrac{\$395,000}{10,000} = \$39.50$	The amount of cash generated from operations for each share of stock.

Net income $250.00

Net income $250.00
Add:
  Depreciation $100,000
  Decrease in accounts
    receivable   50,000
  Increase in accounts payable   15,000
Less:
  Increase in inventory   (20,000)   145,000
Cash from operations $395,000

centered accounting and performance reporting.
Responsibility accounting is based on the assumptions that:

1. All spending can be controlled.
2. Responsibility for spending must be assigned and assigned fairly.

Assigning responsibility in an organization requires that authority to act be clearly assigned and that when responsibilities are assigned, commensurate authority to carry out those responsibilities also be assigned. These relationships are usually presented in the organization's organizational chart and in its chart of accounts. The organizational chart should reflect a plan of organization that provides an appropriate segregation of functional responsibilities. Accounting reports should be prepared to summarize the performance of each responsibility center. Such reports should include only those items over which the center has control (see Exhibit R-4).

Responsibility accounting requires that costs be collected by responsibility centers so that individuals assigned responsibilities can receive appropriate performance reports. Management practice has accepted three major types of responsibility centers:

1. *Expense (or cost) center:* an organizational unit that is held accountable for the incurring of expense.
2. *Revenue center:* an organizational unit that is held accountable for only revenue.
3. *Profit center:* an organizational unit that is held accountable for revenue and expense.
4. *Investment center:* an organization unit whose management is held accountable for attaining a satisfactory rate of return on capital.

Exhibit R-4
Responsibility Accounting Reports

RESPONSIBLE COMPANY
Assembly Shop A
Foreman Report
March 31, 19☐1

	Budget		Actual		Variances Favorable/(Unfavorable)	
Expense	This Mo.	Year to Date	This Mo.	Year to Date	This Mo.	Year to Date
Direct material	$ 15,000	$ 45,000	$ 16,000	$ 50,000	$(1,000)	$ (5,000)
Direct labor	30,000	90,000	25,000	80,000	5,000	10,000
Supplies	5,000	10,000	5,500	12,000	(500)	(2,000)
Other	100,000	250,000	90,000	295,000	10,000	(45,000)
	$150,000	$395,000	$136,500	$437,000	$13,500	$(42,000)

RESPONSIBLE COMPANY
Plant Superintendent: Plant 1
Plant Expense Report
March 31, 19☐1

	Budget		Actual		Variances Favorable/(Unfavorable)	
Expense	This Mo.	Year to Date	This Mo.	Year to Date	This Mo.	Year to Date
Assembly Shop A	$150,000	$ 395,000	$136,500	$ 437,000	$13,500	$(42,000)
Assembly Shop B						
Assembly Shop C			*(Details omitted)*			
Assembly Shop D						
Superintendent's office						
	$500,000	$1,300,000	$490,000	$1,280,000	$10,000	$ 20,000

RESPONSIBLE COMPANY
Vice-President Manufacturing
Expense Report
March 31, 19☐1

	Budget		Actual		Variances Favorable/(Unfavorable)	
Expense	This Mo.	Year to Date	This Mo.	Year to Date	This Mo.	Year to Date
Plant No. 1	$ 500,000	$1,300,000	$ 490,000	$1,280,000	$ 10,000	$ 20,000
Plant No. 2						
Plant No. 3			*(Details omitted)*			
Vice-President's office						
	$3,000,000	$9,300,000	$3,100,000	$9,500,000	$(100,000)	$(200,000)

RESPONSIBLE COMPANY
President
Expense Report
March 31, 19☐1

	Budget		Actual		Variances Favorable/(Unfavorable)	
Department	This Mo.	Year to Date	This Mo.	Year to Date	This Mo.	Year to Date
Manufacturing	$3,000,000	$ 9,300,000	$3,100,000	$ 9,500,000	$(100,000)	$(200,000)
Purchasing						
Sales						
Treasurer			*(Details omitted)*			
Controller						
President's office						
	$9,000,000	$27,700,000	$9,500,000	$28,300,000	$(500,000)	$(600,000)

When profit and investment centers are used, organizations frequently structure themselves in divisions which are responsible for manufacturing and marketing functions. Divisionalization assigns considerable authority and responsibility to division managers. This can improve both the decision-making process and managerial motivation. However, divisionalization can result in unhealthy competition and conflict among division managers so that the welfare of the entire organization is harmed.

The reporting system under responsibility management should be designed so that:

1. each report has a distinct purpose,

2. the reporting system should be reviewed periodically,

3. reports contain only essential information and are kept to a minimum, and

4. reports are accurate, timely, and motivating.

Establishing responsibility for costs, revenues, profits, or investments is difficult to accomplish. General guidelines in this area recommended by a committee of the American Accounting Association recommend that:

1. The person with authority over both the acquisition and use of service should be charged with the cost of such service.

2. The person who can significantly influence the amount of cost through his/her own action can be charged with such cost.

3. A person can be charged with costs that management desires this person to be concerned with even though that individual cannot influence the amount of those costs.

R

If responsibilities are not assigned equitably, the establishment of a responsibility accounting system will be flawed.

See also Planning function; Control function; Organizational behavior; Motivation; Organizing function; Management; Goals and objectives; Decision making; Organizing behavior; Performance evaluation.

REFERENCE
Miller, Elwood L., *Responsibility Accounting and Performance Evaluations* (Van Nostrand Reinhold, Florence, KY, 1982).

RETURN-ON-INVESTMENT ANALYSIS

Return on investment (ROI) is a comprehensive measure of financial performance. The basic formula for computing return on investment involves the following:

ROI = Capital turnover × Margin as a percentage of sales

$$= \frac{\text{Sales}}{\text{Capital employed}} \times \frac{\text{Net income}}{\text{Sales}}$$

The relationship of ROI to balance sheet and income statement items is shown in Exhibit R-2. Note that ROI is computed in this exhibit as follows:

ROI = TURNOVER × EARNING RATIO
where
Turnover = Sales/Capital employed
and
Earning ratio (or Margin) = Net income/Sales

Capital turnover is the ratio of sales to capital employed in generating the sales. Capital turnover is a measure of the use of assets in relation to sales. Generally, the larger the volume of sales that management can generate on a given investment in assets, the more efficient are its operations. Margin is the ratio of net income to sales.

Capital employed can be interpreted to mean (1) total assets, (2) total assets less current liabilities (that is, working capital plus noncurrent assets), or (3) stockholders' equity. When management performance is being evaluated, either the first or second concept of capital employed should be used because management should be held responsible for assets available to them. When stockholders' equity is used as the measure of capital employed, the analysis stresses the long-range ability of the firm to make use of the investments of its owners.

The ROI formula takes into account all of the items that go into the balance sheet and income statement and so represents a comprehensive overview of performance. Exhibit R-5 shows a structural outline of the relationships that make up ROI.

Exhibit R–5
Return-on-Investment Relationships

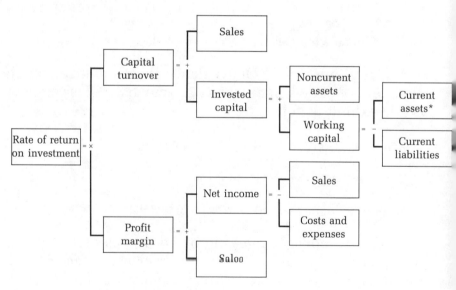

*Includes cash, accounts receivable, and inventory

To illustrate the computation of ROI, assume the following information is available:

Condensed income statement

Sales	$1,000,000
Less: Costs and expenses	800,000
Net income	$ 200,000

From the balance sheet

Working capital	$100,000
Plant and equipment	300,000
Total assets (Invested capital)	$400,000

$$\text{ROI} = \frac{\text{Net income}}{\text{Sales}} \times \frac{\text{Sales}}{\text{Invested capital}}$$

$$= \frac{\$200,000}{\$1,000,000} \times \frac{\$1,000,000}{\$400,000}$$

$$= \frac{\$200,000}{\$400,000}$$

$$= 50\%$$

The ROI formula can be restated as follows:

$$\text{ROI} = \text{Profit margin} \times \text{Capital turnover}$$

$$= 20\% \times 2.5$$

$$= 50\%$$

Various actions can be taken to improve ROI including the following:

1. Increase total sales by increasing volume, sales price, or some combination thereof, while maintaining or improving the margin on sales.

2. Decrease expenses, thereby increasing net income.

3. Reduce the amount of capital employed (for example, reduce the inventory level, improve collection of accounts receivable) without decreasing sales.

If the chief executive officer of this firm wants to increase ROI to 60 percent next year and sales (price and/or volume) and invested capital cannot be changed, what change must occur in net income to achieve this objective?

$$\text{ROI} = 60\% = \frac{\$1,000,000}{\$400,000} \times \frac{\text{Net income (to be computed)}}{\$1,000,000}$$

$$60\% = \frac{\text{Net income}}{\$400,000}$$

Net income = $240,000 (i.e., $400,000 × 60%)

Management must focus attention on profit margin rather than on capital turnover which is assumed to be unchangeable. Since sales cannot be increased, the improvement in net income must come from a reduction of expenses.

Advantages claimed for ROI analysis include the following:

1. Focuses management's attention upon earning the best return on total assets.

2. Serves as a measure of management's efficiency and effectiveness.

3. Integrates financial planning, budgeting, sales objectives, cost control, and profit-making activities.

4. Provides a basis for comparing companies.

5. Provides a motivational basis for management.

6. Identifies weaknesses in the utilization of assets.

See also Ratios; Financial statement analysis; Pricing policy: Return on assets.

REFERENCE
Woelfel, Charles J., and Mecimore, Charles, *The Operating Executive's Handbook of Profit Planning Tools and Techniques* (Probus, Chicago, 1986).

REVENUE

Revenues represent actual or expected cash inflows (or the equivalent) that have occurred or will eventually occur as a result of the enterprise's ongoing major or central operations during the period. Gains are not revenue. Gains are increases in equity (net assets) from peripheral or incidental transactions of an entity and from all other transactions and other events and circumstances affecting the entity during a period except those that result from revenues or investments by owners.

Revenue arises primarily from one or more of the following activities:

1. Selling of products.

2. Rendering services.

3. Permitting others to use the entity's assets (leasing, renting, lending).

4. Disposing of assets other than products.

Recognition is the process of formally recording an item in the financial statements of an entity. Revenues are generally recognized when:

1. the earning process is complete or virtually complete, and

2. an exchange has taken place.

The earning process consists of all those activities that produce revenue, including purchasing, production, selling, delivering, administering, and others.

311

R

Revenue is usually recognized at the time of sale of a product or when services have been rendered. Revenue is sometimes recognized before the point of sale. For example, the percentage-of-completion method is sometimes used to recognize revenue from long-term construction contracts. Some long-term service contracts recognize revenue on the basis of proportional performance. Revenue is sometimes recognized after the point of sale where there is great uncertainty about the collectibility of the receivable involved in a sale. Under such circumstances, revenue can be recognized on the installment method or cost recovery method when cash is collected.

See also Income; Income statement; Elements of financial statements; Financial statements; Measurement.

REFERENCES
SFAC No. 3, *Elements of Financial Statements of Business Enterprises* (FASB, 1981).
SFAC No. 5, *Recognition and Measurement in Financial Statements of Business Enterprises* (FASB, 1984).

S

V

W

$$\boxed{\textbf{S}}$$

SEGMENT PERFORMANCE

A segment of a business is a part of an entity whose activities represent a major line of business or class of customer. A segment is a part of an enterprise that sells primarily to outsiders for a profit. Examples of a segment of a business include a subsidiary, a division, a department, a product, a market, or other separations where the activities, assets, liabilities, and operating income can be distinguished for operational and reporting purposes.

Information about segments of a business, especially for diversified companies, is useful to investors of large, complex, heterogeneous, publicly traded enterprises in evaluating risks, earnings, growth cycles, profit characteristics, capital requirements, and return on investments that can differ among segments of a business. The need for segment information is the result of many environmental factors including the growth of conglomerates, acquisitions, diversifications, and foreign activities of enterprises.

A reportable segment is determined by the following procedures:

1. Identifying the enterprise's products and services.

315

S

2. Grouping the products and services into industry segments.

3. Selecting the significant industry segments by applying various tests established for this purpose.

Segment information that must be disclosed in financial statements includes an enterprise's operations in different industries, foreign operations and export sales, and major customers. Detailed information must be disclosed relating to revenues, segment's operating profit or loss, and identifiable assets along with additional information. Segment information is primarily a disaggregation of the entity's basic financial statements.

See also Planning function; Control function; Performance evaluation.

REFERENCE
SFAS No. 14, *Financial Reporting for Segments of a Business Enterprise* (FASB, 1976).

VARIANCES

A variance is the difference between actual and standard or between budgeted and actual expenditures or expenses. Variance analysis is based on the concept of management by exception. A variance system provides management with information only when conditions, performance, or activity varies from what they should be. Variance systems are designed and used primarily for control and evaluation purposes. An effective variance system would focus on matters which require management's attention. Variance analysis is also widely used to evaluate performance.

Variance systems typically require:

1. accurate performance standards or benchmarks,

2. variables that are subject to control,

3. accurate measurement procedures for inputs and outputs, and

4. responsibilities assignable, preferably through responsibility centers.

Actual cost can differ from standard or budgeted cost because (1) the actual price or rate differs from the standard or budgeted and (2) actual usage or efficiency differs from the standard or budgeted. A price or rate variance indicates that more or less was paid for the cost factor than the standard or budgeted required. A usage or efficiency variance indicates that more or less of the cost factor was used than was anticipated by the standard or budgeted.

See also Cost Accounting Systems; Gross margin analysis; Organizational behavior; Performance evaluation; Control function; Distribution cost control; Goals and objectives; Management; Organizational behavior; Distribution cost control.

REFERENCE
Anthony, Robert N., and Welsch, Glenn A., *Fundamentals of Management Accounting* (Irwin, Homewood, IL, 1984).

WORKING CAPITAL

Working capital is the excess of current assets over current liabilities. The amount of working capital is computed by subtracting current liabilities from current assets. Current assets include those resources that are in the form of cash and those that are reasonably expected to be sold, consumed, or converted into cash during the normal operating cycle of the business or within one year if the operating cycle is shorter than one year. The normal operating cycle of a business is the average time it takes to convert cash into inventory, sell the inventory, and collect the receivables. Current liabilities are obligations that are to be paid, liquidated, or settled with current assets.

Working capital is useful in determining the ability of the firm to finance current operations and to meet obligations as they mature. Adequate working capital is necessary for a business if it is to operate efficiently and effectively.

Working capital management is often the most critical factor for business firms. Liquidity is crucial to survival and success. Short-term credit must be obtained usually through trade credit, but this can be costly if discounts are not taken. The areas of finance that are of utmost importance to small firms include the following:

1. reliance on internal financing, especially through profits retained in the business, or funds supplied by owners.

2. reliance on financial controls, especially financial ratios and trend and variance analysis.

3. reliance on working capital management so that limited resources are efficiently and effectively employed.

Firms typically pass through four stages in their life cycles:

1. *Experimental period.* Sales and profits grow slowly. Financing comes primarily from the personal savings of the owners, trade credit, and, in some cases, from government agencies. Growth rate is accelerating, product lines are usually limited, and market share is often volatile.

2. *Exploitation period.* Sales and profits grow more quickly as the firm's products and services gain acceptance. Financing comes primarily from internal financing by owners, trade credit from suppliers, bank credit, and venture capital. Management's goal is to prolong this stage of the cycle. Product lines increase rapidly and market share fluctuates.

3. *Maturity.* Sales growth slows down. Product or service demand declines. The company may go public at this point and turn to the money and capital markets for funds. Product lines do not change in any significant way and market share is stable.

4. *Aging or decline.* During this phase, competition and substitute products and services appear, the demand for the firm's products or services is saturated, and technological and managerial obsolescence occurs. Diversification, mergers, and consolidations become a major part of the financial packaging. Managers strive to delay this phase of the life cycle.

The four stages of the life cycle of a business are conceptualized in Exhibit W.1.

Exhibit W–1
Life Cycle of a Typical Business

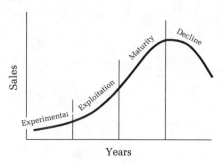

See also Liquidity; Cash management; Cash budget; Forecasting financial requirements; Financial statement analysis; Ratios.

REFERENCE
Woelfel, Charles J., and Mecimore, Charles D., *The Operating Executive's Guide to Profit Planning Tools and Techniques* (Probus Publishing Co., Chicago, 1986).